I0016421

RANJOT SINGH CHAHAL

Bitcoin Mastering for Beginners

Your Comprehensive Cryptocurrency Guide and Beyond

Rana Books

First published by Rana Books UK 2023

Copyright © 2023 by Ranjot Singh Chahal

First edition

ISBN: 978-81-19786-05-3

Contents

I

Part 1: The Value of Bitcoin

The value of Bitcoin is driven by a complex interplay of market sentiment, adoption, and speculative trading.

1

Understanding Cryptocurrency

1.1 What is Bitcoin?

Bitcoin is one of the most well-known and widely used cryptocurrencies in the world. It was created in 2009 by an anonymous person or group of people using the pseudonym Satoshi Nakamoto. Bitcoin is a decentralized digital currency that operates on a peer-to-peer network without the need for a central authority such as a government or financial institution. It is based on cryptographic principles making it secure and resistant to counterfeiting.

Bitcoin can be used for various purposes including online trans-actions investment or as a store of value. Bitcoin transactions are recorded on a public ledger called the blockchain which ensures transparency and security. Bitcoin can be acquired by purchasing it through exchanges mining (the process of validating transactions and adding them to the blockchain or as payment for goods and services.

1.2 Brief History of Bitcoin

Bitcoin's history is filled with milestones and significant events that have shaped its growth and adoption. Here are some key highlights:

- 2008: The concept of Bitcoin was introduced in Satoshi Nakamoto's whitepaper titled "Bitcoin: A Peer-to-Peer Electronic Cash System."

- 2009: The first ever Bitcoin block known as the Genesis Block was mined by Nakamoto marking the creation of the Bitcoin network. Bitcoin's value was initially insignificant and it was mainly individual enthusiasts and early adopters who started using it.

- 2010: Bitcoin gained its first notable valuation when a user traded 10000 bitcoins for two pizzas in what became known as the "Bitcoin Pizza Day." This transaction highlighted the concept of using Bitcoin as a medium of exchange.

- 2011: Bitcoin saw significant media attention and experienced its first major price increase reaching a peak of $31 per bitcoin. However it also faced security concerns and negative publicity due to incidents like the hacking of the Mt. Gox exchange.

- 2013: Bitcoin entered a phase of intense growth reaching a peak price of over $1000. This was fueled by increased media coverage growing acceptance by merchants and the entrance of institutional investors.

- 2017: Bitcoin witnessed its most dramatic price surge to date reaching almost $20000 per bitcoin. This attracted mainstream attention and sparked a global interest in cryptocurrencies and blockchain technology.

- 2020: Bitcoin gained further recognition as a hedge against economic uncertainties with institutional investors and companies like MicroStrategy and Tesla investing heavily in the cryptocurrency.

1.3 Other Cryptocurrencies
   Bitcoin paved the way for the development of various other cryptocurrencies known as altcoins (alternative coins). Here are some examples of other significant cryptocurrencies:

- Ethereum (ETH): Launched in 2015 Ethereum is a decentralized platform that enables developers to build and deploy smart contracts and decentralized applications (dapps). Ether (ETH) is its native cryptocurrency.

- Ripple (XRP): Ripple is both a cryptocurrency and a digital payment protocol. It aims to provide fast low-cost international money transfers using blockchain technology.

- Litecoin (LTC): Created in 2011 Litecoin is often referred to as the "silver" to Bitcoin's "gold." It offers faster transaction confirmation times and a different hashing algorithm.

- Bitcoin Cash (BCH): Bitcoin Cash is a result of a hard fork from Bitcoin in 2017. It aims to address some of Bitcoin's scalability issues by increasing the block size.

- Cardano (ADA): Cardano is a blockchain platform that aims to provide a secure and scalable infrastructure for the development of decentralized applications. ADA is its native cryptocurrency.

These are just a few examples among thousands of cryptocurrencies available today. Each cryptocurrency often serves a specific purpose or targets a different niche providing a variety of options for those interested in participating in the digital currency ecosystem.

1.4 Blockchain Technology

Blockchain technology is a fundamental innovation that underpins the operation of cryptocurrencies like Bitcoin. A blockchain is a decentralized and distributed digital ledger that records transactions across multiple computers or nodes. Here are the key features of blockchain technology:

- Decentralization: The blockchain operates on a peer-to-peer network eliminating the need for a central authority. This makes it resilient to single points of failure and censorship as transactions are verified and recorded by multiple participants.

- Transparency: The entire transaction history is stored on the blockchain which can be viewed by anyone. This transparency ensures accountability and discourages fraudulent activities.

- Security: Transactions on the blockchain are secured using cryptographic algorithms. Once a transaction is recorded on the blockchain it becomes immutable and tamper-proof making it highly secure.

- Consensus Mechanisms: Blockchain networks rely on consensus mechanisms to validate transactions and add them to the ledger. There are various consensus protocols such as Proof of Work (PoW) and Proof of Stake (PoS which ensure the accuracy and integrity of the blockchain.

- Smart Contracts: Smart contracts are self-executing contracts with predefined rules written in code. They automate the execution of agreements and transactions eliminating the need for intermediaries.

The potential applications of blockchain technology extend beyond cryptocurrencies. It can be utilized in various industries such as supply chain management healthcare finance and voting systems. Blockchain technology can enhance transparency streamline processes reduce costs and increase trust and security in various sectors.

1.5 Advantages and Disadvantages of Cryptocurrency
    Cryptocurrencies offer several advantages but they also come with their disadvantages. Let's explore them in detail:

Advantages:
    - Decentralization: Cryptocurrencies operate on decentralized networks reducing the reliance on central authorities and enabling peer-to-peer transactions. This promotes financial inclusivity and empowers individuals to have full control of their money.

- Security: Cryptocurrencies use cryptographic algorithms that make transactions highly secure. The decentralized nature of blockchain technology also mitigates the risk of hacking and fraud.

- Anonymity: While not all cryptocurrencies offer complete anonymity they often provide a level of pseudonymity that allows users to maintain privacy. This can be beneficial in regions with strict financial regulations or jurisdictions with concerns about privacy.

- Accessibility: Cryptocurrencies can be accessed by anyone with an internet connection regardless of their location banking status or identity. This can empower the unbanked population to participate in the global economy.

- Potential for High Returns: Cryptocurrencies have the potential for high returns on investment. Early investors in Bitcoin for example have seen significant gains over the years.

Disadvantages:
   - Volatility: Cryptocurrencies are known for their price volatility. Rapid price fluctuations can lead to significant gains or losses in a short period. This volatility can make cryptocurrencies risky and unsuitable for risk-averse individuals.

- Regulatory Uncertainty: The regulatory landscape for cryptocurrencies is still evolving in many jurisdictions. This uncertainty can result in conflicting regulations making it challenging for businesses and individuals to navigate the space.

- Lack of Consumer Protection: Unlike traditional financial systems cryptocurrencies often lack the same level of consumer protection measures. Fraud scams and theft can occur and there may be limited recourse for affected individuals.

- Energy Consumption: Some cryptocurrencies such as Bitcoin require substantial computational power leading to high energy consumption. This has raised concerns about the environmental sustainability of cryptocurrencies.

- Scalability Limitations: As cryptocurrencies gain popularity scalability becomes a significant challenge. Bitcoin for example has faced scalability issues resulting in slower transaction processing times and higher fees during peak periods.

In conclusion cryptocurrency especially Bitcoin has revolutionized the financial industry by introducing a decentralized and secure digital currency system. Alongside Bitcoin numerous other cryptocurrencies and blockchain applications have emerged. While cryptocurrencies offer advantages such as decentralization security and accessibility they also come with disadvantages including volatility regulatory uncertainty and scalability issues. As the technology continues to evolve it is essential to weigh the benefits and drawbacks to make informed decisions regarding cryptocurrency use and investment.

2

Factors Influencing the Value of Bitcoin

The value of Bitcoin is influenced by a multitude of factors, with supply and demand dynamics at the forefront. Market sentiment plays a pivotal role, with positive news and widespread optimism driving its price upwards, while negative sentiment can lead to sharp declines. Regulatory developments and government interventions also exert significant influence, as changes in laws and policies can affect investor confidence and market stability. Additionally, macroeconomic factors such as inflation, economic crises, and geopolitical events can impact Bitcoin's perceived value as a store of value and hedge against traditional financial risks. Lastly, technological advancements, network security, and adoption trends further contribute to the complex ecosystem shaping Bitcoin's value in the ever-evolving cryptocurrency market.

2.1 Supply and Demand:

The supply and demand dynamics play a significant role in determining the value of Bitcoin. Bitcoin has a limited supply with a total of 21 million coins that can ever exist. This scarcity contributes to its value as it creates a sense of digital gold. The rate at which new coins are created known as the Bitcoin halving reduces the supply over time and can influence the price.

Similarly the demand for Bitcoin is driven by various factors. As more people recognize the potential of Bitcoin as a store of value or a medium of exchange the demand increases. Factors such as increasing institutional adoption global economic uncertainties and inflation concerns can drive higher demand for Bitcoin which can lead to price appreciation.

2.2 Market Sentiment and Speculation:

The sentiment and speculation in the market can significantly impact the value of Bitcoin. Bitcoin is known for its price volatility which often attracts traders investors and speculators. Positive news or announcements related to Bitcoin such as large corporations or notable investors publicly supporting or investing in Bitcoin can create positive market sentiment increasing demand and driving up prices. Conversely negative news such as regulatory crackdowns or security breaches can induce fear and cause prices to decline.

Furthermore speculation also plays a role in the value of Bitcoin. Traders and investors engage in speculation by buying or selling Bitcoin based on their expectations of future price movements. Speculative activities can introduce additional volatility into the market as traders react to perceived opportunities for profits.

2.3 Adoption and Use Cases:

The adoption of Bitcoin as a medium of exchange and its use cases in various industries can influence its value. When more businesses and merchants accept Bitcoin as a form of payment it increases the utility and demand for the cryptocurrency. This increased adoption can contribute to the value appreciation of Bitcoin as it becomes more widely accepted and recognized as a viable alternative to traditional currencies.

Moreover the emergence of innovative use cases and applications built on top of the Bitcoin blockchain can also impact its value. For example the development of decentralized finance (DeFi) platforms or non-fungible tokens (NFTs) that utilize the Bitcoin network can attract more users and increase demand for Bitcoin.

2.4 Regulatory Environment:
The regulatory environment both domestically and internationally can have a significant impact on the value of Bitcoin. Governments and regulatory bodies have varying stances on cryptocurrencies and any regulatory developments or changes can influence market sentiment and adoption.

Positive regulatory measures such as the recognition of Bitcoin as a legal payment method or the introduction of clear guidelines for cryptocurrency businesses can boost confidence in the market and attract institutional investors. Conversely negative regulatory actions such as bans or stricter regulations can create uncertainty and hinder the widespread acceptance and use of Bitcoin potentially leading to a decrease in value.

2.5 Economic and Geopolitical Factors:
Economic and geopolitical factors can also impact the value of Bitcoin. In times of economic instability or hyperinflation

individuals and institutions may turn to Bitcoin as a hedge against traditional fiat currencies. For example during the COVID-19 pandemic the global economy experienced significant turbulence and the unprecedented monetary stimulus measures taken by central banks led to concerns about inflation. These factors led to increased interest in Bitcoin as a store of value contributing to its price appreciation.

Geopolitical events such as trade wars political tensions or economic sanctions can also affect the value of Bitcoin. In regions where there are restrictions on capital movement or a lack of trust in traditional financial systems individuals may turn to Bitcoin as a means to bypass these limitations. As a result the demand for Bitcoin can increase causing its value to rise.

In conclusion the value of Bitcoin is influenced by a variety of factors. Supply and demand dynamics market sentiment and speculation adoption and use cases the regulatory environment and economic and geopolitical factors all play a role in determining the value of the cryptocurrency. Understanding these factors and their interplay is crucial for anyone interested in investing or participating in the Bitcoin market.

3

Bitcoin as a Store of Value

Bitcoin's role as a store of value is multifaceted and influenced by various factors. Its scarcity, with a capped supply of 21 million coins, creates an appealing narrative akin to digital gold, attracting investors seeking a hedge against inflation and traditional financial risks. Market sentiment also plays a pivotal role, as confidence in Bitcoin's store of value properties can drive demand and price appreciation. Regulatory developments and institutional adoption are critical too, as they validate Bitcoin's legitimacy as a long-term store of wealth. Additionally, network security and technological advancements bolster its credibility as a secure and resilient store of value in the digital age, while ongoing adoption trends contribute to its evolving status in the broader financial landscape.

3.1 Digital Gold: Bitcoin vs Traditional Assets

Bitcoin is often referred to as digital gold due to its similarities with traditional assets used as stores of value such as gold. Both gold and Bitcoin share certain characteristics that make them attractive as a long-term investment and a hedge against economic uncertainties.

One similarity is scarcity. Gold has limited supply in the earth's crust and the rate of its extraction is relatively stable. Similarly Bitcoin has a limited supply of 21 million coins with a predetermined issuance schedule. This limited supply makes both assets resistant to inflationary pressures.

Another similarity is their decentralized nature. Gold is not controlled by any central authority or government whereas Bitcoin operates on a decentralized network called blockchain. The decentralized nature of both gold and Bitcoin provides an alternative to traditional fiat currencies that are subject to government control and manipulation.

Both assets can also be easily divisible and portable. Gold can be melted down and divided into smaller pieces while Bitcoin can be divided into small units called satoshis. Additionally Bitcoin can be sent or stored digitally allowing for ease of transfer and storage especially in the digital age.

When comparing Bitcoin to traditional assets like stocks and bonds one key difference is their correlation to other markets. Traditional assets are often tied to the performance of global economies and can be affected by factors such as interest rates government policies and market sentiment. Bitcoin on the other hand has shown limited correlation to traditional assets making it a potential diversification tool in an investment portfolio.

For example during the 2008 financial crisis many traditional assets experienced significant declines. However Bitcoin was still in its early stages at that time and had yet to establish itself as a store of value. In more recent years Bitcoin has demonstrated its ability to act independently from traditional markets providing investors with an alternative asset class that may perform differently during market downturns.

3.2 Inflation Hedge

One of the key reasons why Bitcoin is considered a store of value is its potential as an inflation hedge. Inflation refers to the increase in the general price level of goods and services over time eroding the purchasing power of fiat currencies. When inflation occurs the value of traditional currency decreases making it less effective as a store of value.

Bitcoin with its limited supply and decentralized nature offers an alternative form of currency that is resistant to inflation. The maximum supply of 21 million coins ensures that new Bitcoins are issued at a decreasing rate with the final coin expected to be mined around the year 2140. This scarcity feature protects its value against the potential debasement of fiat currencies due to inflationary policies.

During times of economic volatility and uncertainty investors often seek assets that can retain or increase in value. Bitcoin's limited supply and decentralized nature make it an attractive option for those looking to hedge against inflationary pressures or economic downturns.

For example in countries experiencing hyperinflation such as

Venezuela and Zimbabwe citizens have turned to Bitcoin as a potential solution. By converting their local currency into Bitcoin they are able to protect their wealth from the rapid devaluation of their fiat currency.

3.3 Bitcoin's Limited Supply

One of the key factors that make Bitcoin a store of value is its limited supply. As mentioned earlier there will only ever be 21 million Bitcoins in existence with a predetermined issuance schedule. This limited supply creates scarcity similar to gold and can potentially drive up its value over time.

The issuance of new Bitcoins occurs through a process called mining. Miners use specialized hardware to solve complex mathematical problems and in return they are rewarded with newly minted Bitcoins. However the number of new Bitcoins issued decreases over time following a halving event that occurs approximately every four years.

This halving event cuts the block reward miners receive in half. In the early days of Bitcoin the block reward was 50 Bitcoins but it has since been reduced to 6.25 Bitcoins per block. The decreasing issuance rate acts as a mechanism to control the rate at which new Bitcoins enter the market ultimately leading to a finite supply.

The limited supply of Bitcoin creates scarcity and can potentially increase its value over time. This is in contrast to traditional fiat currencies which can be printed by central banks to meet economic demands. The ability to mint new Bitcoins is fixed and cannot be influenced by any central authority making it immune to manipulation and inflationary pressures.

3.4 Security and Audibility

Another aspect that bolsters Bitcoin's role as a store of value is its security and audibility. Bitcoin operates on a decentralized network called the blockchain which serves as a public ledger containing all transaction history.

The blockchain provides transparency and immutability ensuring that transactions cannot be altered or reversed once recorded. This feature enhances the trustworthiness of Bitcoin as a store of value as it eliminates the need for intermediaries and ensures the integrity of the transaction history.

Furthermore the security of Bitcoin is maintained through cryptographic techniques such as public-key cryptography. Each Bitcoin address is associated with a unique pair of cryptographic keys: a public key and a private key. The private key is kept secret by the owner of the Bitcoin address and is used to sign transactions while the public key is used to verify the authenticity of transactions.

The use of cryptographic keys makes Bitcoin highly secure from unauthorized access or tampering. As long as the private key remains secure the Bitcoin stored in a specific address is safe from being spent by anyone else.

Additionally the decentralized nature of the Bitcoin network provides added security. Unlike traditional banking systems which rely on a single point of failure the decentralized network ensures that there is no single point of vulnerability. This means that even if one part of the network is compromised the overall integrity of the system remains intact.

Overall the combination of security measures such as blockchain technology and cryptographic techniques enhance Bitcoin's ability to serve as a reliable and secure store of value.

In conclusion Bitcoin is increasingly being recognized as a store of value due to its similarities to traditional stores of value such as gold its potential as an inflation hedge its limited supply and its security and audibility features. Bitcoin's decentralized nature limited supply and resistance to inflation provide investors with an alternative asset class that can retain or increase in value over time. As with any investment it is important to conduct thorough research and consider the risks associated with Bitcoin before making any investment decisions.

4

Bitcoin as a Medium of Exchange

Bitcoin's function as a medium of exchange is influenced by a range of factors. Its decentralized nature and global accessibility make it an attractive option for cross-border transactions, potentially reducing transaction costs and delays. The scalability of the Bitcoin network, including its processing speed and fees, plays a vital role in determining its efficiency as a medium of exchange. Regulatory frameworks and government acceptance can either facilitate or hinder its adoption for everyday transactions, while market sentiment and merchant acceptance also impact its usage. Moreover, ongoing developments in blockchain technology and layer-two solutions like the Lightning Network contribute to Bitcoin's potential to serve as a practical medium of exchange, although challenges such as price volatility still need to be addressed for widespread adoption in this role.

4.1 Merchant Adoption

Merchant adoption refers to the acceptance of Bitcoin by businesses as a method of payment for goods and services. In order for Bitcoin to function effectively as a medium of exchange it needs to be widely accepted by merchants.

Over the years the adoption of Bitcoin by merchants has grown significantly. Many businesses both online and offline have started accepting Bitcoin as a payment option alongside traditional payment methods. This is particularly true in industries such as e-commerce travel and service-based businesses.

One of the key advantages for merchants in accepting Bitcoin is the reduction in transaction fees compared to traditional payment processors. Bitcoin transactions generally have lower fees especially for cross-border payments. This can be beneficial for businesses especially those with international customers or suppliers.

Another advantage for merchants is the elimination of chargebacks. Chargebacks occur when customers dispute a transaction and the funds are taken back from the merchant. Bitcoin transactions are irreversible making them immune to chargebacks. This reduces the risk for merchants particularly in industries with a higher incidence of fraudulent chargebacks.

Merchant adoption of Bitcoin can also provide businesses with a marketing advantage. By accepting Bitcoin businesses can cater to a niche market of Bitcoin users who prefer to use their digital assets for transactions. This can attract new customers who are specifically looking to spend their Bitcoin. Additionally accepting Bitcoin can be seen as a sign of technological innovation and forward-thinking which may attract tech-savvy customers.

4.2 Payment Processors and Wallets

To facilitate Bitcoin transactions payment processors and wallets have emerged as intermediaries between merchants and consumers. These services make it easier for merchants to accept Bitcoin payments and for consumers to transact with Bitcoin.

Payment processors act as intermediaries by providing the necessary tools and infrastructure for merchants to accept Bitcoin payments. They handle the technical aspects of processing Bitcoin transactions and convert them into the local currency if desired by the merchant. Some popular Bitcoin payment processors include BitPay CoinGate and Coinbase Commerce.

Wallets on the other hand are digital wallets that allow users to store send and receive Bitcoin. Similar to a physical wallet a Bitcoin wallet is a software application that securely stores the user's private keys which are used to access and control their Bitcoin. Wallets come in various forms including mobile wallets desktop wallets and hardware wallets.

Payment processors often integrate with wallets allowing users to make payments directly from their Bitcoin wallets. This seamless integration makes it convenient for consumers to spend their Bitcoin at participating merchants.

4.3 Bitcoin Transactions: Speed and Cost

The speed and cost of Bitcoin transactions are critical factors in determining its viability as a medium of exchange. Let's explore how Bitcoin transactions work and how they compare to traditional payment methods.

When a Bitcoin transaction is initiated it is broadcasted to the entire network of participants. Miners who are responsible for validating and confirming transactions include the transaction in a new block of the blockchain. This confirmation process can take some time especially during periods of high network congestion.

The speed of Bitcoin transactions also depends on the transaction fee paid by the sender. Miners prioritize transactions with higher fees so including a higher fee can expedite the confirmation process. However it's worth noting that even with a high fee Bitcoin transactions can still take several minutes to be confirmed.

In terms of cost Bitcoin transactions generally have lower fees compared to traditional payment methods especially for cross-border transactions. Traditional payment processors often charge a percentage fee for each transaction which can be significant for large or frequent transactions. Bitcoin transaction fees on the other hand are typically a fixed amount based on the size of the transaction in bytes.

However it's important to consider the volatility of Bitcoin's exchange rate when assessing the cost of Bitcoin transactions. Since the value of Bitcoin can fluctuate considerably businesses and consumers need to factor in potential price swings when transacting with Bitcoin.

4.4 Cross-Border Transactions

One area where Bitcoin shines as a medium of exchange is cross-border transactions. Traditional cross-border transactions can be complex costly and time-consuming due to the involvement of intermediary banks and multiple currency conversions.

Bitcoin eliminates the need for intermediaries in cross-border transactions. Since Bitcoin operates on a decentralized network transactions can be conducted directly between parties without the involvement of traditional banking systems. This reduces the complexity and cost associated with cross-border payments.

With Bitcoin cross-border transactions can also be faster compared to traditional methods. The speed at which Bitcoin transactions are processed is not impacted by borders or time zones which means that payments can be made and received instantly regardless of the distance between the sender and the receiver.

Additionally the lower transaction fees of Bitcoin can make it a more cost-effective solution for cross-border payments. Traditional payment processors often charge hefty fees for international transactions including foreign exchange fees and intermediary fees. Bitcoin transactions on the other hand typically have lower fixed fees making them more affordable for cross-border transfers.

4.5 Bitcoin's Role in Financial Inclusion

Financial inclusion refers to the accessibility and availability of financial services to individuals who are traditionally under-served by the banking system. Bitcoin has the potential to play a significant role in enhancing financial inclusion particularly in regions where access to banking services is limited.

Bitcoin enables individuals to have full control over their finances without the need for a traditional bank account. All that is required is access to the internet and a Bitcoin wallet. This accessibility allows individuals who are unbanked or underbanked to participate in the global economy engage in commerce and store value.

In countries with unstable economies or inflationary currencies Bitcoin can provide a stable alternative for individuals to preserve their wealth. By storing their funds in Bitcoin individuals can protect themselves from the devaluation of their national currency.

Remittances which are cross-border money transfers from migrants to their home countries are another area where Bitcoin can enhance financial inclusion. Traditional remittance services are often expensive with high fees and slow processing times. Bitcoin can streamline the remittance process by enabling low-cost and instant transfers directly between individuals.

For example a migrant worker earning Bitcoin in one country can send Bitcoin to their family back home who can then convert it to the local currency or use it to make purchases. This eliminates the need for costly intermediaries and provides a more efficient way for funds to reach their intended recipients.

However it's worth noting that Bitcoin's adoption and impact on financial inclusion are still limited in some areas. Adoption barriers such as infrastructure requirements technological literacy and regulatory challenges can hinder widespread use of Bitcoin as a medium of exchange particularly in developing economies. Nonetheless the underlying technology and principles behind Bitcoin hold promise for improving financial inclusion in the future.

In conclusion Bitcoin has emerged as a viable medium of exchange with increasing merchant adoption payment processors facilitating transactions and wallets providing storage and transfer capabilities. Bitcoin transactions offer advantages such as lower fees elimination of chargebacks and faster cross-border transfers. Additionally Bitcoin has the potential to enhance financial inclusion by providing individuals with access to financial services and facilitating low-cost remittances. While adoption and acceptance of Bitcoin still face challenges its use as a medium of exchange holds promise for the future of global commerce.

II

Part 2: Investing in Bitcoin

Investing in Bitcoin carries both potential for high returns and significant risks due to its volatility and regulatory uncertainties.

5

Evaluating Bitcoin as an Investment

Bitcoin the first decentralized cryptocurrency has gained significant attention as an investment option over the past decade. As with any investment it is essential to evaluate the potential risks and rewards associated with investing in Bitcoin. In this section we will explore various factors to consider when evaluating Bitcoin as an investment including risk versus reward analysis portfolio diversification long-term versus short-term investing fundamental analysis and technical analysis.

5.1 Risk vs Reward Analysis

Risk and reward are essential components of any investment endeavor and evaluating the risk versus reward profile of Bitcoin is crucial. Bitcoin's unique characteristics as a decentralized digital currency give it both potential rewards and risks.

One of the primary rewards of investing in Bitcoin is its potential for high returns. Bitcoin has experienced significant price appreciation over the years with some investors making substantial profits. For instance from its initial price of a few cents per coin in 2010 Bitcoin reached an all-time high of nearly $65000 per coin in April 2021.

However Bitcoin also comes with inherent risks. One significant risk is its price volatility. The price of Bitcoin can experience rapid and dramatic fluctuations within short periods. For example in 2017 Bitcoin reached an all-time high of nearly $20000 only to crash to around $3000 within a year. Such price swings can lead to substantial losses for investors.

Additionally Bitcoin is still a relatively new asset class and its future is uncertain. Regulatory challenges technological advancements and market acceptance are all factors that can influence the value and sustainability of Bitcoin. Therefore investors must carefully assess these risks and evaluate whether the potential rewards outweigh them.

5.2 Portfolio Diversification

Diversification is a risk management strategy that involves spreading investments across different assets to reduce exposure to any single investment's risk. When evaluating Bitcoin as an investment it's important to consider its role within a well-diversified portfolio.

Bitcoin's unique characteristics as a decentralized digital asset make it a compelling option for portfolio diversification. While traditional investment assets such as stocks and bonds are affected by factors like economic conditions and central bank policies Bitcoin operates independently. This lack of correlation with traditional assets gives Bitcoin the potential to serve as a hedge against inflation and a diversification tool.

However it's essential to note that diversification does not elimi-nate risk entirely. Although Bitcoin may provide diversification benefits it also introduces its own set of risks. Therefore in-vestors should carefully consider their risk tolerance and ensure that their portfolios are appropriately balanced across different assets including both traditional and alternative investments.

5.3 Long-term vs Short-term Investing

One critical consideration when evaluating Bitcoin as an in-vestment is the desired investment timeframe and strategy. Investors can approach Bitcoin investment from a long-term or short-term perspective each with its own benefits and risks.

Long-term investing in Bitcoin involves buying and holding the cryptocurrency for an extended period often several years or more. This strategy aims to capture potential long-term price appreciation and benefits from Bitcoin's scarcity and growing adoption. Long-term investors typically believe in the fundamental value proposition of Bitcoin and its potential as a store of value and medium of exchange.

Short-term investing in Bitcoin involves taking advantage of short-term price movements and attempting to profit from market volatility. Traders employing this strategy may engage in technical analysis and trading techniques to buy low and sell high within shorter timeframes. Short-term investing requires a deep understanding of market dynamics and carries higher risks due to market uncertainties and price fluctuations.

Both long-term and short-term investing approaches in Bitcoin have their pros and cons. Long-term investing can be more aligned with the principles of hodling (holding on for dear life) and benefiting from potential long-term price appreciation. Short-term investing can provide opportunities to capitalize on short-term price movements but it requires active monitoring and a higher tolerance for market volatility.

Ultimately the choice of investment timeframe and strategy should align with an investor's financial goals risk tolerance and investment expertise.

5.4 Fundamental Analysis

Fundamental analysis involves evaluating an asset's intrinsic value based on various factors such as financial performance underlying assets and market conditions. When evaluating Bitcoin as an investment several fundamental factors can provide insights into its potential value.

One important fundamental factor for Bitcoin is its limited supply. The maximum supply of Bitcoin is capped at 21 million coins ensuring scarcity. This limited supply feature is often cited as a reason for potential price appreciation over time as demand increases.

Another fundamental factor to consider is the growing adoption and acceptance of Bitcoin. Bitcoin has gained traction as a means of payment with various merchants and businesses accepting it as a form of payment. Additionally institutional investors and financial institutions have started to embrace Bitcoin which can further contribute to its adoption and value.

Regulatory factors also play a crucial role in evaluating Bitcoin's fundamental value. The regulatory landscape for cryptocurrencies is evolving with governments and regulatory bodies worldwide implementing rules and regulations. Favorable regulations can provide a more secure environment for Bitcoin while strict regulations or bans can negatively impact its adoption and value.

Moreover developments in blockchain technology scalability and security enhancements are also fundamental factors to consider when evaluating Bitcoin's potential long-term value. Technological advancements can impact Bitcoin's usability transaction speed and security which in turn can influence its adoption and value.

Fundamental analysis is a comprehensive process that requires examining multiple factors and understanding their potential impact on Bitcoin's value. It can help investors gain insights into Bitcoin's long-term prospects and its overall position within the broader investment landscape.

5.5 Technical Analysis

Technical analysis involves studying past price and volume data as well as charts and patterns to forecast future price movements. Although controversial technical analysis can be a valuable tool in evaluating Bitcoin's short-term price trends and identifying potential entry and exit points for traders.

Various technical analysis tools and indicators are used in analyzing Bitcoin's price movements. Some commonly used indicators include moving averages relative strength index (RSI and Bollinger Bands. These indicators help identify trends overbought or oversold conditions and potential price reversal points.

Chart patterns such as triangles head and shoulders or double tops provide insights into market sentiment and potential future price movements. Traders often analyze these patterns and use them to make short-term trading decisions.

It's important to note that technical analysis is not a fool-proof method for predicting Bitcoin's price movements. The cryptocurrency market is highly volatile and influenced by various factors including market sentiment news events and investor behavior. Therefore technical analysis should be used in conjunction with other forms of analysis and risk management strategies.

In conclusion evaluating Bitcoin as an investment involves considering various factors such as risk versus reward portfolio diversification investment timeframe fundamental analysis and technical analysis. Bitcoin presents potential rewards including high returns and portfolio diversification benefits. However it also carries risks including price volatility and uncertain regulatory factors. Investors should carefully evaluate these factors align their investment strategy with their financial goals and risk tolerance and consider Bitcoin's fundamental and technical aspects to make informed investment decisions.

6

Investing in Bitcoin: Key Considerations

In recent years Bitcoin has gained significant popularity as a form of investment. As with any investment it is essential to consider various factors before diving into the world of Bitcoin. This section will deep dive into some key considerations when it comes to investing in Bitcoin including choosing a cryptocurrency exchange wallet security dollar-cost averaging tax considerations and managing risks and volatility.

6.1 Choosing a Cryptocurrency Exchange

Before investing in Bitcoin one of the primary steps is to choose a reliable cryptocurrency exchange. A cryptocurrency exchange is an online platform that allows users to buy sell and trade cryptocurrencies including Bitcoin. It's crucial to consider factors such as ease of use security measures reputation fees and available trading pairs when selecting an exchange.

Ease of use: Look for an exchange with a user-friendly interface making it easy for you to navigate and execute trades without any technical difficulties.

Security measures: Cryptocurrency exchanges are often tar-geted by hackers due to the potential for large amounts of value stored in hot wallets. Look for exchanges that implement robust security measures such as two-factor authentication (2FA cold storage options and encryption protocols to protect your funds.

Reputation: Research the reputation of the exchange by reading user reviews checking if it is regulated in the relevant jurisdic-tion and looking for any previous security breaches or incidents that may have occurred.

Fees: Consider the fee structure of the exchange for deposits withdrawals and trading activities. Some exchanges have a flat fee while others have a percentage-based fee which can significantly impact your profitability.

Trading pairs: Check whether the exchange offers a wide range of trading pairs including Bitcoin to fiat currencies (e.g USD EUR) and other cryptocurrencies. This ensures you have flexibility in trading and can easily convert your Bitcoin into other assets if desired.

Some popular cryptocurrency exchanges to consider are Coin-base Binance Kraken and Gemini. However it is essential to conduct thorough research and evaluate each exchange based on your specific needs and preferences.

6.2 Wallet Security: Hot vs. Cold Storage

Once you have purchased Bitcoin on an exchange it is crucial to consider how you will store your investment. Wallet security is of utmost importance as it ensures the safety of your Bitcoin holdings. There are two main types of wallets: hot wallets and cold storage.

Hot wallets are digital wallets connected to the internet and are typically provided by cryptocurrency exchanges. They provide convenient access to your Bitcoin holdings for trading or transferring purposes. However they are more vulnerable to hacking attempts as they are constantly connected to the internet.

Cold storage wallets on the other hand are not connected to the internet making them less susceptible to hacking attempts. They come in various forms such as hardware wallets (physical devices paper wallets (printed or written-down private and public keys and offline software wallets.

It is generally recommended to store the majority of your Bitcoin holdings in cold storage wallets and only keep a smaller amount in hot wallets for frequent trading or transactions. This way even if the hot wallet is compromised the majority of your funds will remain secure.

When selecting a cold storage wallet it is vital to consider factors such as ease of use robust security features backup and recovery options and compatibility with different operating systems. Popular cold storage wallets include Ledger Nano X Trezor Model T and KeepKey.

Remember to keep your wallet's backup information such as recovery seeds or private keys in a secure location and consider utilizing a strong password or passphrase to protect your wallet.

6.3 Dollar-Cost Averaging

Bitcoin's price is notoriously volatile often experiencing significant price swings in short periods. Dollar-cost averaging (DCA) is an investment strategy that can help mitigate the impact of price volatility over time.

DCA involves regularly investing a fixed amount of money into Bitcoin at regular intervals regardless of its price. By doing so you buy more Bitcoin when prices are lower and fewer when prices are higher effectively averaging out the cost per coin over time.

For example suppose you decide to invest $500 in Bitcoin every month. In a month when the price is high your $500 will buy fewer Bitcoins but in a month when the price is low your $500 will buy more Bitcoins. Over time this strategy can reduce the impact of short-term price movements and potentially generate more favorable overall returns.

DCA is a popular strategy for long-term Bitcoin investors who believe in the potential of Bitcoin but want to minimize the potential risks associated with its volatility.

6.4 Tax Considerations

Investing in Bitcoin can have tax implications and it is essential to understand the tax laws and regulations in your jurisdiction.

In many countries including the United States Bitcoin is treated as property for tax purposes. This means that any gains or losses from Bitcoin investments may be subject to capital gains tax. The tax rates can vary depending on the duration of the investment (short-term or long-term) and the individual's tax bracket.

It is advisable to consult with a tax professional or accountant who specializes in cryptocurrency taxation to ensure you are compliant with the tax laws in your jurisdiction. They can provide guidance on reporting your Bitcoin investments calculating capital gains or losses and any relevant tax deductions or exemptions.

Additionally keeping detailed records of your Bitcoin transactions including the date of acquisition purchase price sale price and any transaction fees can be crucial for accurate tax reporting.

6.5 Managing Risks and Volatility

Bitcoin is known for its volatility which presents both opportunities and risks for investors. To effectively manage risks associated with Bitcoin investments consider the following strategies:

Diversification: Avoid putting all your investment capital into Bitcoin alone. Diversify your portfolio by investing in a range of assets such as stocks bonds real estate or other cryptocurrencies.

Diversification helps spread the risk across different asset classes and can potentially reduce the impact of Bitcoin's volatility.

Risk tolerance: Understand your risk tolerance level and align your investment decisions accordingly. Investing in Bitcoin involves a certain level of risk and it is important to invest only what you can afford to lose. Consider your financial goals time horizon and risk appetite before making any investment decisions.

Research and education: Stay informed about the latest trends news and developments in the cryptocurrency market. Understanding the fundamentals of Bitcoin its technology and potential use cases can help you make more informed investment decisions. Engage in thorough research and consider credible sources before making any investment choices.

Setting realistic expectations: Bitcoin's price history has seen significant highs and lows and it is crucial to set realistic expectations regarding potential returns. While Bitcoin has shown substantial growth over the years it is important to remember that past performance does not guarantee future results. Be mindful of market cycles and avoid making impulsive investment decisions based solely on short-term price movements.

Regular portfolio assessments: Continuously monitor and reassess your investment portfolio. Set predefined parameters for profit-taking and stop-loss levels. Regularly reviewing your portfolio and making adjustments based on your investment goals and market conditions can help ensure your investment strategy remains aligned with your objectives.

Conclusion

Investing in Bitcoin can be a rewarding endeavor but it also requires careful consideration and risk management. Choosing a reliable cryptocurrency exchange securing your Bitcoin wallet through cold storage utilizing dollar-cost averaging to mitigate volatility understanding tax considerations and managing risks effectively are all critical components of a successful Bitcoin investment strategy. By following these key considerations and applying a disciplined approach you can navigate the world of Bitcoin investing with greater confidence. Remember to conduct thorough research seek professional advice if needed and always stay informed to make well-informed investment decisions.

7

Alternative Investment Options

Alternative investment options encompass a diverse range of assets and strategies, with several factors influencing their attractiveness. Investor sentiment and risk appetite play a significant role, as some alternatives, like venture capital or private equity, can offer potentially high returns but come with substantial risk. Economic conditions, such as interest rates and inflation, affect the appeal of assets like real estate or commodities, which are often considered hedges against traditional market fluctuations. Regulatory changes and tax considerations impact the viability of options like cryptocurrencies or art investments. Furthermore, the expertise required and liquidity constraints can influence an investor's choice among alternative assets, making due diligence and a diversified portfolio critical in navigating this complex landscape.

7.1 Bitcoin Investment Trusts and Funds:

Bitcoin investment trusts and funds offer individuals and institutions the opportunity to invest in Bitcoin without directly purchasing and storing the cryptocurrency themselves. These investment vehicles pool money from investors and allocate it to Bitcoin assets.

One popular example is the Grayscale Bitcoin Trust (GBTC). GBTC is a publicly traded trust that holds Bitcoin assets and allows investors to gain exposure to Bitcoin's price movements without actually owning the cryptocurrency. Investors can buy shares of GBTC through brokerage accounts similar to buying shares of a stock.

The advantage of investing in Bitcoin through trusts and funds is that it provides investors with a convenient and regulated way to gain exposure to the cryptocurrency market. It eliminates the need for investors to set up a digital wallet and store their Bitcoin securely. Additionally these investment vehicles may offer tax advantages and professional management.

However it's important to note that investing in Bitcoin through trusts and funds comes with its own set of risks. The price of the trust or fund may not always closely track the price of Bitcoin itself due to factors such as fees and premiums. Additionally investors do not have direct control over their Bitcoin holdings as the trust or fund is managed by third-party entities.

7.2 Bitcoin Mining:

Bitcoin mining is the process by which new Bitcoins are created and transactions are verified on the Bitcoin network. Miners use specialized hardware and software to solve complex mathematical problems that validate and secure transactions.

Individuals and businesses can participate in Bitcoin mining by setting up their own mining rigs or by joining mining pools. Mining rigs consist of powerful computers equipped with specialized mining hardware such as ASIC (Application-Specific Integrated Circuit) chips. These rigs work to solve mathematical problems and are rewarded with newly minted Bitcoins for their efforts.

Bitcoin mining can be a profitable investment option if done correctly but it requires significant upfront investment in mining equipment and ongoing operational costs such as electricity and cooling. The profitability of mining is also dependent on the price of Bitcoin and the overall network difficulty.

It's worth noting that Bitcoin mining has become highly competitive over the years and individuals with consumer-grade hardware may find it challenging to compete with large-scale mining operations. As a result many miners join mining pools where resources are pooled together to increase the chances of earning rewards.

7.3 Initial Coin Offerings (ICOs):

Initial Coin Offerings (ICOs) are fundraising events in the cryptocurrency industry where new tokens or coins are sold to investors in exchange for established cryptocurrencies such as Bitcoin or Ethereum or even fiat currencies.

ICOs gained popularity during the cryptocurrency boom of 2017 as a way for startups to raise funds for their projects. Investors would purchase tokens during the ICO hoping that the project's value would increase leading to a profitable investment.

ICOs can offer high returns on investment but they also come with significant risks. Many ICOs turned out to be scams or failed projects leaving investors with worthless tokens. Regulatory concerns and lack of investor protection were also prevalent during the ICO boom.

While ICOs have declined in popularity due to increased regulatory scrutiny they remain an alternative investment option for those willing to take on higher risks and conduct thorough due diligence on the projects before investing.

7.4 Decentralized Finance (DeFi):

Decentralized Finance or DeFi refers to the use of blockchain technology and cryptocurrencies to recreate traditional financial systems and services in a decentralized and permissionless manner. It aims to eliminate intermediaries such as banks and financial institutions and provide open and transparent financial services.

DeFi encompasses a wide range of applications and services including decentralized lending and borrowing platforms decentralized exchanges stablecoins yield farming and liquidity pools. These platforms allow users to lend or borrow cryptocurrencies trade assets directly earn interest on deposits and participate in various investment strategies.

One notable example of DeFi is the platforms built on the Ethereum blockchain which use smart contracts to automate and enforce financial agreements. Users can interact with these platforms using wallets and decentralized applications (dApps) without the need for intermediaries.

Investing in DeFi can provide investors with opportunities for high returns as well as the ability to participate in innovative financial services. However DeFi investments also come with risks including smart contract vulnerabilities price volatility of underlying assets and regulatory uncertainties.

7.5 Non-Fungible Tokens (NFTs):

Non-Fungible Tokens (NFTs) are unique digital assets that represent ownership or proof of authenticity of a specific item or piece of content. Unlike cryptocurrencies such as Bitcoin which are interchangeable and have the same value NFTs are unique and cannot be substituted for one another.

NFTs have gained significant attention in recent years particularly in the world of digital art and collectibles. Artists and creators can tokenize their digital works and sell them as NFTs providing proof of ownership and creating a new market for digital assets.

Investing in NFTs can offer potential returns particularly in the art world where rare and sought-after digital artworks can sell for significant sums. Additionally NFTs provide artists and creators with new revenue streams and the ability to monetize their digital creations directly.

However it's important to be aware of the risks associated

with investing in NFTs. The market for NFTs can be highly speculative with significant price volatility and potential for market bubbles. There are also concerns about copyright infringement plagiarism and the long-term value of digital assets.

Conclusion:

Alternative investment options in the cryptocurrency space continue to evolve offering investors diverse opportunities to participate in the digital asset ecosystem. Bitcoin investment trusts and funds provide a convenient way to gain exposure to Bitcoin without directly owning and managing the cryptocurrency. Bitcoin mining allows individuals and businesses to contribute to the network's operations while potentially earning rewards.

Initial Coin Offerings (ICOs) offer investors the chance to invest in new cryptocurrency projects although they come with higher risks and regulatory considerations. Decentralized Finance (DeFi) platforms provide permissionless and decentralized financial services enabling users to lend borrow trade and invest in cryptocurrencies. Non-Fungible Tokens (NFTs) represent ownership of unique digital assets such as art and collectibles creating new opportunities for investors and content creators.

As with any investment it's crucial to conduct thorough research assess risks and consider personal financial goals and risk tolerance before engaging in alternative investment options in the cryptocurrency space.

III

Part 3: Learning and Staying Informed

Learning and staying informed about Bitcoin is essential for making informed decisions in the ever-evolving cryptocurrency space.

8

Educational Resources for Cryptocurrency

Educational resources for cryptocurrency are essential for individuals looking to understand and invest in this rapidly evolving field. These resources are influenced by several factors. Firstly, the comprehensiveness and credibility of the information provided matter greatly. Investors seek resources that offer clear explanations of blockchain technology, cryptocurrency fundamentals, and trading strategies from reputable sources. Accessibility is also a key factor, with the availability of free or affordable educational materials making it more inclusive. Regulatory changes and industry developments impact the relevance and timeliness of these resources, as cryptocurrency is subject to evolving rules and market trends. Additionally, community engagement and peer-reviewed content contribute to the effectiveness of these resources in empowering individuals to make informed decisions in the crypto space.

8.1 Books Blogs and Podcasts

Books blogs and podcasts are invaluable educational resources for learning about cryptocurrency. They provide in-depth insights analysis and expert opinions on various aspects of the cryptocurrency world. Here are some examples:

Books:

1. "Mastering Bitcoin: Unlocking Digital Cryptocurrencies" by Andreas M. Antonopoulos: This book is considered a cornerstone in understanding the technical aspects of Bitcoin and blockchain technology.

2. "The Age of Cryptocurrency: How Bitcoin and the Blockchain Are Challenging the Global Economic Order" by Paul Vigna and Michael J. Casey: This book explores the impact of Bitcoin and blockchain technology on the traditional financial system.

Blogs:

1. CoinDesk: CoinDesk is a leading cryptocurrency news and analysis platform providing up-to-date information on the latest trends developments and regulations in the crypto world.

2. The Coinbase Blog: Coinbase is one of the most popular cryptocurrency exchanges and their blog covers a wide range of topics such as beginner's guides market insights and new coin listings.

Podcasts:

1. "Unchained" by Laura Shin: This podcast features interviews with top industry experts providing deep insights into the world of blockchain cryptocurrencies and decentralized finance.

2. "The Pomp Podcast" by Anthony Pompliano: In this podcast Pompliano discusses cryptocurrencies investing and financial markets with various industry leaders.

8.2 Online Courses and Tutorials

Online courses and tutorials offer structured educational programs for individuals looking to gain practical knowledge and skills in cryptocurrency. These courses cover a wide range of topics from beginner-level introductions to advanced trading strategies. Here are some examples:

1. "Cryptocurrency Investment Course 2021: Fund Your Retirement!" on Udemy: This course teaches the fundamentals of investing in cryptocurrencies and explores various investment strategies to achieve long-term financial goals.

2. "Blockchain Basics" on Coursera: This course provides a comprehensive introduction to blockchain technology covering its history structure and various use cases.

3. "Technical Analysis Academy: Introduction to Cryptocurrency Trading" on YouTube: This tutorial series covers technical analysis techniques specifically for cryptocurrency trading helping traders understand market trends and make informed investment decisions.

8.3 Bitcoin and Cryptocurrency Communities

Being part of online communities centered around Bitcoin and cryptocurrencies can provide valuable insights and opportunities for learning. These communities often consist of passionate individuals who share knowledge discuss market trends and provide support. Here are some examples of popular Bitcoin and cryptocurrency communities:

1. Reddit - r/Bitcoin: This subreddit is dedicated to discussions related to Bitcoin. It serves as a platform for users to ask questions share news and engage in debates about the cryptocurrency.

2. Bitcointalk: Bitcointalk is one of the oldest and largest online Bitcoin forums. It covers a wide range of topics including technical discussions mining trading and development of blockchain-based projects.

3. Crypto Twitter: Twitter has become a hub for cryptocurrency discussions with many influential figures in the industry sharing their insights news and analysis. Following key individuals and participating in relevant discussions can be an excellent way to stay updated.

8.4 Networking and Conferences

Networking and attending cryptocurrency conferences provide opportunities for learning connecting with industry professionals and staying updated on the latest trends. These events often feature keynote speeches panel discussions interactive workshops and networking sessions. Here are some notable cryptocurrency conferences:

1. Consensus: Consensus is one of the largest annual blockchain

conferences organized by CoinDesk. It brings together industry leaders developers investors and policymakers to discuss the future of cryptocurrencies and blockchain technology.

2. Blockchain Expo: Blockchain Expo is a series of global conferences focused on blockchain and its real-world applications. They feature expert speakers panel discussions and exhibitions related to blockchain technology and cryptocurrencies.

8.5 Industry News and Research

Staying informed through industry news and research provides critical insights into the rapidly evolving cryptocurrency landscape. Here are some reputable sources for current news and research:

1. CoinMarketCap: CoinMarketCap is a popular cryptocurrency market analysis platform that tracks the prices market caps and trading volumes of various cryptocurrencies. It also provides news educational articles and research reports.

2. Cointelegraph: Cointelegraph is a leading cryptocurrency news platform that covers a wide range of topics including market analysis regulatory developments and industry trends.

3. Messari: Messari is a research platform that offers in-depth analysis data and insights on cryptocurrencies and blockchain projects. Its research reports provide valuable information for investors and industry professionals.

In conclusion there are numerous educational resources available for individuals interested in learning about cryptocurrency. Books blogs and podcasts offer in-depth analysis and expert opinions. Online courses and tutorials provide structured learning programs while crypto communities networking events and conferences allow for interaction and networking. Finally staying informed through industry news and research is crucial for understanding the dynamic world of cryptocurrencies. By leveraging these educational resources individuals can expand their knowledge and make informed decisions in the cryptocurrency space.

9

Understanding Crypto Market Trends

Understanding crypto market trends is crucial for investors and enthusiasts in the cryptocurrency space, and it relies on various factors. Market sentiment plays a significant role, as positive news and widespread optimism can lead to bullish trends, while negative sentiment can trigger bearish trends. Technological developments within the cryptocurrency ecosystem, such as up-grades or innovations in blockchain technology, can influence market trends by affecting the utility and adoption of specific cryptocurrencies. Regulatory changes and government policies can have a profound impact, either boosting confidence and driving adoption or causing market uncertainty. Additionally, macroeconomic factors like global economic conditions and inflation can shape trends as investors seek alternatives to traditional assets. Lastly, the behavior of whales and large institutional investors can also sway market trends, making it crucial to monitor their activities and sentiments in the crypto space.

9.1 Bull and Bear Markets:

The cryptocurrency market is known for its highly volatile nature characterized by frequent price fluctuations. It experiences two main market trends: bull markets and bear markets.

Bull Market: A bull market is characterized by a sustained upward price movement where the overall sentiment is optimistic and investors have confidence in the market. During a bull market prices tend to rise steadily or even experience exponential growth. As a result investors are more likely to buy and hold cryptocurrencies hoping to profit from further price appreciation.

For example Bitcoin experienced a significant bull market from 2016 to early 2018 where its price surged from around $400 to nearly $20000. This rapid increase in value attracted a lot of attention and triggered a massive influx of new investors and projects in the cryptocurrency space.

Bear Market: In contrast a bear market refers to a prolonged period of declining prices and pessimistic sentiment in the market. During bearish phases prices can experience significant drops investor confidence diminishes and fear dominates the market.

An example of a bear market is the crypto winter that occurred from late 2018 to early 2019 where Bitcoin's price dropped from its all-time high of $20000 to around $3000. Many other cryptocurrencies experienced similar declines during this period.

9.2 Market Cycles and Timing:

Cryptocurrency market cycles are the repeated patterns of bull and bear markets over time. These cycles can vary in length and understanding them can help traders and investors anticipate the market's direction and make informed decisions.

Timing the market refers to trying to predict when the market will switch from a bull to a bear market or vice versa. While it is challenging to time the market accurately understanding market cycles can provide useful insights.

One popular theory in the cryptocurrency space is the "Four-Year Cycle" or the "Bitcoin Halving Cycle." Bitcoin goes through a halving event approximately every four years which reduces the block rewards for miners and effectively lowers the rate of new Bitcoin issuance. These halvings are believed to trigger bull markets because they reduce the supply of new Bitcoin entering the market while demand remains constant or increases.

For example Bitcoin experienced its first halving event in November 2012 which was followed by a significant bull market in 2013. The second halving occurred in July 2016 leading to the famous bull run of 2017. The most recent halving took place in May 2020 and Bitcoin's price surged to new all-time highs in 2021.

Although market cycles provide historical patterns they are not foolproof indicators and other factors such as market sentiment and fundamental analysis should also be considered when making investment decisions.

9.3 Sentiment Analysis and Market Psychology:

Sentiment analysis and market psychology play a crucial role in understanding cryptocurrency market trends. The sentiment refers to the overall attitude or emotions of market participants towards a particular cryptocurrency or the market as a whole.

Sentiment analysis involves monitoring and analyzing social media channels news articles forums and other sources of information to gauge how people feel about a specific cryptocurrency. Positive sentiment often indicates that investors are optimistic leading to increased buying pressure and potentially driving the price up. Conversely negative sentiment can lead to selling pressure and price declines.

Market psychology refers to the collective mindset and behavior of market participants. Emotional factors such as fear greed and uncertainty can heavily influence decision-making and ultimately drive market trends. For instance during a bull market investors might exhibit a fear of missing out (FOMO leading to buying frenzies and further price appreciation. On the other hand during a bear market fear can dominate leading to panic selling and further price declines.

Understanding sentiment analysis and market psychology requires keeping an eye on market sentiment indicators sentiment analysis tools and staying informed about the latest news and developments in the cryptocurrency space.

9.4 Technical Indicators and Chart Patterns:

Technical analysis involves studying historical price data and using various indicators and chart patterns to predict future price movements. While technical analysis may not provide definitive predictions it can help investors identify potential trends and make more informed decisions.

Technical Indicators: There are numerous technical indicators used in cryptocurrency trading. Some popular ones include moving averages (MA relative strength index (RSI MACD (Moving Average Convergence Divergence Bollinger Bands and Fibonacci retracements.

Moving averages help smooth out price data and identify trend directions. For example using a 50-day and 200-day moving average if the 50-day moving average crosses above the 200-day moving average it is considered a bullish signal.

RSI is a momentum oscillator that measures the speed and change of price movements. An RSI above 70 indicates overbought conditions suggesting a potential reversal or correction in price. Conversely an RSI below 30 suggests oversold conditions indicating a potential price recovery.

Chart Patterns: Chart patterns represent recognizable and repeatable patterns in price charts that can provide insights into market trends and potential future price movements. Some commonly recognized chart patterns include head and shoulders double tops double bottoms triangles and flags.

Head and shoulders patterns for example often indicate a trend reversal from bullish to bearish. It consists of three peaks with the middle peak (the head) being higher than the other two (the shoulders). A breakdown below the neckline (a line connecting the lows of the two shoulders) suggests a potential price decline.

It's important to note that technical indicators and chart patterns are not foolproof and should be used in conjunction with other analysis methods. It's recommended to combine them with fundamental analysis sentiment analysis and risk management strategies for a comprehensive approach to trading.

9.5 Risk Management Strategies:

Managing risk is a crucial aspect of trading or investing in cryptocurrencies as the market's volatility can result in significant gains or losses. Here are some risk management strategies to consider:

Diversification: Diversifying your cryptocurrency portfolio can help mitigate risk by spreading your investments across different assets. By investing in a variety of cryptocurrencies you decrease the reliance on a single asset's performance.

Stop Loss Orders: Implementing stop-loss orders can help protect your investment from significant losses. A stop-loss order is an instruction to sell a cryptocurrency if its price falls to a certain predetermined level limiting your potential losses.

Position Sizing: Position sizing involves determining how much capital to allocate to each trade or investment. By defining a percentage of your portfolio to risk per trade you avoid putting too much capital at stake in a single trade reducing the overall risk exposure.

Research and Education: Educating yourself about cryptocurrencies understanding the technology and staying updated on market trends and news can enable you to make more informed decisions and mitigate risks.

Technical Analysis: Utilizing technical analysis tools and indicators can help identify potential entry and exit points enabling you to set more appropriate stop-loss levels and manage risk effectively.

In conclusion understanding cryptocurrency market trends involves analyzing bull and bear markets identifying market cycles and timing considering sentiment analysis and market psychology utilizing technical indicators and chart patterns and implementing risk management strategies. While no method can guarantee success combining these approaches can provide a more comprehensive understanding of the market and improve decision-making. Remember to continuously educate yourself stay informed and adapt your strategies to evolving market conditions.

10

The Future of Bitcoin and Cryptocurrency

The future of Bitcoin and cryptocurrency is a topic of great interest and speculation, shaped by numerous factors. Technological advancements will continue to influence their development, with potential improvements in scalability, security, and energy efficiency being pivotal for mainstream adoption. Regulatory decisions and government policies will play a critical role in determining the regulatory landscape, affecting investor confidence and market stability. Institutional adoption and integration into traditional financial systems could solidify cryptocurrencies' place in the global economy. Market sentiment and public perception will continue to sway prices and usage patterns, while macroeconomic factors like inflation and economic crises may drive increased interest in cryptocurrencies as hedges against traditional financial risks. The ongoing evolution of blockchain technology and innovative use cases will further shape the future of these digital assets, making it a dynamic and evolving space to watch.

10.1 Regulatory Outlook:

The regulatory landscape for Bitcoin and cryptocurrency is evolving. Governments and regulatory bodies worldwide are grappling with how to regulate these digital assets effectively. Initially there was skepticism and concerns regarding the potential for illicit activities such as money laundering and terrorism financing. However as the technology matures and gains wider acceptance regulators are starting to develop frameworks to govern the industry.

Different countries have taken different approaches to regulate cryptocurrencies. Some have imposed strict regulations while others have opted for more lenient approaches. For example countries like Japan and Switzerland have implemented regulations with licensing requirements for cryptocurrency exchanges providing a legal framework for businesses to operate in. On the other hand countries like Malta and Singapore have embraced cryptocurrency-friendly regulations to attract blockchain startups to their jurisdictions.

The future regulatory outlook for Bitcoin and cryptocurrency will likely involve a balance between fostering innovation and protecting investors and consumers. As the industry continues to grow governments will refine their regulatory frameworks to ensure adequate oversight without stifling innovation.

10.2 Institutional Adoption:

Institutional adoption of Bitcoin and cryptocurrency has been gaining momentum in recent years. Traditional financial institutions such as banks and asset management firms are increasingly exploring opportunities in the crypto space. This development indicates a growing acceptance of digital assets as a legitimate investment class.

Institutional investors are attracted to Bitcoin and cryptocurrency for various reasons. First they see it as a hedge against traditional financial markets and inflation. Second the potential for high returns in a rapidly evolving industry is enticing. Finally blockchain technology itself has applications beyond cryptocurrencies such as supply chain management and decentralized finance (DeFi making it a strategic investment for businesses.

The entry of institutional investors into the cryptocurrency market brings increased liquidity stability and credibility. It also opens up new avenues for retail investors to participate leading to further growth and adoption. As more institutional players enter the space it is likely that they will exert significant influence on the market dynamics and regulatory landscape.

10.3 Central Bank Digital Currencies (CBDCs):

Central bank digital currencies (CBDCs) are digital forms of national fiat currencies issued by central banks. Unlike decentralized cryptocurrencies like Bitcoin CBDCs are centralized and issued by government authorities. CBDCs aim to leverage blockchain technology and provide a digital alternative to physical cash.

The concept of CBDCs has gained traction globally. Several countries including China Sweden and the Bahamas are actively exploring or piloting CBDC projects. These digital currencies can offer benefits such as improved financial inclusion increased efficiency in payment systems and better traceability of transactions.

The introduction of CBDCs raises questions about the future of cryptocurrencies like Bitcoin. While some argue that CBDCs could compete with cryptocurrencies others believe that they can coexist. Cryptocurrencies offer features like decentralization privacy and censorship resistance that CBDCs may not provide. Additionally cryptocurrencies have established networks and user communities which can give them a competitive advantage.

The extent of CBDC adoption and their impact on the crypto market will depend on various factors such as public trust government policies and interoperability with existing blockchain networks. It is an emerging area that will shape the future of monetary systems and digital currencies.

10.4 Scalability and Network Upgrades:

Scalability has been a long-standing challenge for Bitcoin and other cryptocurrencies. The ability to handle a high volume of transactions quickly and cost-effectively is crucial for widespread adoption and everyday use.

Bitcoin's original blockchain has faced limitations in terms of transaction throughput leading to congestion and high fees during periods of high demand. To address this various scaling solutions have been proposed and implemented such as Segregated Witness (SegWit) and the Lightning Network.

SegWit improves transaction efficiency by separating signature data from transaction data allowing for more transactions to be stored in a single block. This upgrade has already been adopted by a significant portion of the Bitcoin network increasing its scalability.

The Lightning Network is a layer-2 protocol built on top of the Bitcoin blockchain. It enables off-chain transactions allowing for fast and low-cost transactions between participating users. By moving the majority of transactions off-chain the Lightning Network can significantly increase Bitcoin's transaction capacity.

In addition to these upgrades new cryptocurrencies and blockchain networks have emerged that prioritize scalability from the outset. For example Ethereum 2.0 aims to address scalability issues with the introduction of a new consensus mechanism called Proof-of-Stake (PoS) and shard chains which will increase the network's capacity.

Scalability continues to be a focus of research and development in the cryptocurrency community. As technical advancements are made and implemented cryptocurrencies have the potential to compete with traditional payment networks in terms of speed cost and scalability.

10.5 Impact of Emerging Technologies:

Emerging technologies such as artificial intelligence (AI Internet of Things (IoT and blockchain have the potential to shape the future of Bitcoin and cryptocurrency in various ways.

AI can improve the efficiency and security of cryptocurrency transactions. For example AI algorithms can analyze the vast amount of transaction data to detect patterns and anomalies associated with fraudulent activities. AI can also be used for sentiment analysis predicting market trends and optimizing investment strategies in the cryptocurrency market.

IoT can enable new use cases for cryptocurrencies such as connected devices autonomously transacting with each other using cryptocurrencies as a medium of exchange. For instance smart homes equipped with IoT devices could automatically pay for utilities or services using cryptocurrencies eliminating the need for traditional payment systems.

Blockchain itself is an emerging technology with significant potential. Beyond cryptocurrencies blockchain can be used for various applications including supply chain management identity verification voting systems and decentralized finance (DeFi). These use cases can revolutionize existing industries and create new economic ecosystems.

The integration of these emerging technologies with cryptocurrencies can unlock new possibilities and drive innovation in the crypto space. However it also poses challenges including privacy concerns security risks and regulatory implications.

In conclusion the future of Bitcoin and cryptocurrency is multi-faceted and subject to various factors including regulatory developments institutional adoption CBDCs scalability and emerging technologies. The regulatory landscape is gradually maturing with governments seeking a balance between oversight and fostering innovation. Institutional adoption brings credibility and liquidity to the market while CBDCs raise questions about the role of cryptocurrencies. Scalability upgrades and emerging technologies like AI IoT and blockchain continue to push the boundaries of what cryptocurrencies can achieve. The future of Bitcoin and cryptocurrency is undoubtedly exciting and will continue to evolve as new technologies and use cases emerge.

IV

Part 4: Bitcoin and Security

Bitcoin's security relies on its decentralized blockchain technology and cryptographic principles, making it resilient against many traditional threats, but individual users must take precautions to protect their private keys and wallets.

11

Securing Your Bitcoin Holdings

11. Securing Your Bitcoin Holdings

Bitcoin being a digital currency comes with its own set of security concerns. The decentralized nature of the blockchain makes it imperative for individuals to take necessary precautions to protect their Bitcoin holdings. In this section we will explore various measures and best practices for securing your Bitcoin.

11.1 Private Keys and Public Addresses:
   Private keys and public addresses are at the core of Bitcoin security. A private key is a unique alphanumeric code that allows you to access and control your Bitcoin holdings. A public address on the other hand is a derivative of the private key and serves as your public identity on the blockchain.

It is vital to keep your private keys secure to prevent unauthorized access to your Bitcoins. Here are some guidelines for safeguarding your private keys:

a) Use a Hardware Wallet: Hardware wallets are physical devices designed specifically for storing private keys offline. They offer enhanced security by keeping your keys offline and require physical confirmation for transactions. Examples of popular hardware wallets include Ledger and Trezor.

b) Use a Cryptocurrency Wallet: Cryptocurrency wallets such as mobile or desktop wallets store private keys on your device. While convenient they are more susceptible to malware attacks or device compromise. Be sure to choose a reputable wallet provider and regularly update your wallet software.

c) Paper Wallets: A paper wallet is a physical printout of your private and public keys. It is considered one of the most secure methods as it keeps your keys offline. However caution must be exercised as paper wallets are prone to physical damage and must be kept in a safe place.

11.2 Two-Factor Authentication (2FA):

Two-Factor Authentication (2FA) adds an extra layer of security during the login process. It requires users to provide two pieces of evidence to gain access to their Bitcoin holdings. The first factor is usually a password while the second factor can be a verification code sent to your mobile device or generated by an authenticator app.

Enabling 2FA on your Bitcoin exchange accounts online wallets or any other services you use to manage your Bitcoin is highly recommended. It significantly reduces the risk of unauthorized access even if your password is compromised.

Examples of popular 2FA methods include Google Authenticator Authy and hardware tokens like YubiKey.

11.3 Multisignature Wallets:

Multisignature (multisig) wallets require multiple private keys to authorize a Bitcoin transaction. This adds an additional layer of security as it prevents a single person or device from having complete control over your funds. Instead a predetermined number of signatures are required to validate a transaction.

For example you can set up a 2-of-3 multisig wallet where three private keys are generated: one held by you one by a trusted friend and one by a trusted third-party service provider. Any two out of the three keys are required to authorize a transaction reducing the risk of a single point of failure.

Multisig wallets are available on various platforms including hardware wallets and certain cryptocurrency wallet applications.

11.4 Cold Storage Best Practices:

Cold storage refers to keeping your Bitcoin holdings offline away from internet-connected devices. This method provides the highest level of security as it eliminates the risk of hacking or malware attacks. Here are some best practices for implementing cold storage:

a) Hardware Wallets: As mentioned earlier hardware wallets are excellent for cold storage. They store your private keys securely on the device keeping them offline and protected from potential online threats.

b) Creating an Offline Wallet: An offline wallet can be generated on an air-gapped computer disconnected from the internet. The private and public keys are created offline minimizing the risk of exposure to hackers. However caution must be exercised during the setup process to ensure the offline environment is secure.

c) Paper Wallets: Paper wallets as discussed earlier are an effective cold storage solution. Generate a paper wallet on a device that is not connected to the internet and keep multiple copies in secure physically accessible locations.

d) Secure Storage: Regardless of the method used it is crucial to store your cold storage wallets securely. Consider using a safe or a safety deposit box in a bank to protect your wallets from physical damage or theft. Back up your wallet information in multiple locations to prevent loss.

11.5 Protecting Against Scams and Phishing:

The rising popularity of Bitcoin has attracted scammers and phishing attempts. It is essential to stay vigilant and be aware of common scams to protect your Bitcoin holdings. Here are some tips to avoid falling victim to scams:

a) Verify the Source: Make sure you are interacting with legitimate and trusted sources when making Bitcoin transactions or accessing your Bitcoin holdings. Double-check URLs email addresses and digital signatures to ensure security.

b) Be Cautious of Phishing Attempts: Phishing attempts involve fraudsters posing as trusted entities to trick you into providing your private keys or login credentials. Be skeptical of unsolicited emails or messages that ask for your personal information. Always double-check the credibility of the sender before taking any action.

c) Educate Yourself: Stay informed about the latest scams and phishing techniques prevalent in the Bitcoin ecosystem. Keep up-to-date with security best practices and use reputable sources for information.

d) Regularly Update Software: Keep your Bitcoin wallets devices and associated software up to date with the latest security patches. Regularly updating your software ensures that known vulnerabilities are patched reducing the risk of exploitation.

In conclusion securing your Bitcoin holdings requires a combination of best practices and cautious behavior. By following the guidelines for protecting private keys implementing two-factor authentication utilizing multisignature wallets adopting cold storage methods and being aware of scams and phishing attempts you can significantly enhance the security of your Bitcoin investments. Remember to always prioritize security and regularly educate yourself about the evolving threats and best practices in the Bitcoin ecosystem.

12

Legal and Regulatory Compliance

Ensuring legal and regulatory compliance in the cryptocurrency space is imperative and involves several key considerations. Firstly, it's essential to understand the specific regulations applicable in your jurisdiction, as they can vary significantly from one place to another. Complying with Know Your Customer (KYC) and Anti-Money Laundering (AML) requirements when dealing with exchanges or financial institutions is a fundamental obligation. Staying up-to-date with tax regulations related to cryptocurrency transactions, including reporting and capital gains tax, is crucial to avoid legal issues. Additionally, be aware of any licensing requirements for businesses or individuals operating in the cryptocurrency industry. Regularly monitoring and adapting to changes in regulatory frameworks is essential to ensure ongoing compliance and mitigate legal risks. Engaging legal counsel with expertise in cryptocurrency law can provide valuable guidance in navigating this complex regulatory landscape.

12.1 Taxation of Cryptocurrency:

The taxation of cryptocurrency is an important aspect of legal and regulatory compliance. Cryptocurrency is considered a digital asset for tax purposes and its taxation varies from country to country. In general there are two main areas of taxation when it comes to cryptocurrency: capital gains tax and income tax.

Capital gains tax is applied when you sell or exchange cryptocurrency for a profit. The taxable amount is calculated by subtracting the cost basis (the amount you paid to acquire the cryptocurrency) from the sale proceeds. The resulting amount is then subject to the applicable capital gains tax rate.

For example let's say you bought 1 Bitcoin for $10000 and later sold it for $15000. In this scenario your capital gain would be $5000 ($15000 - $10000). Depending on the tax laws in your country you would need to report and pay capital gains tax on this amount.

Income tax is relevant when you receive cryptocurrency as payment for goods or services or when you mine or receive it through other forms of acquisition. In such cases the fair market value of the cryptocurrency received is considered taxable income and needs to be reported accordingly.

For instance if you are a freelancer who receives 0.5 Bitcoin as payment for a project the fair market value of that Bitcoin at the time of receipt needs to be determined and reported as income on your tax return.

It's important to note that tax regulations surrounding cryptocurrency can be complex and subject to change. Therefore it's advisable to consult with a tax professional or accountant who specializes in cryptocurrency to ensure you comply with the specific tax laws in your jurisdiction.

12.2 Reporting Requirements:

In addition to taxation there are reporting requirements that individuals and businesses must fulfill when dealing with cryptocurrency. These requirements primarily focus on providing transparency and combating illicit activities such as money laundering and terrorist financing.

One of the key reporting requirements is the obligation to report cryptocurrency transactions exceeding a certain threshold. This threshold varies from country to country. For example in the United States any individual or business that receives more than $10000 worth of cryptocurrency in a single transaction or a series of related transactions must file a Report of Foreign Bank and Financial Accounts (FBAR) with the Financial Crimes Enforcement Network (FinCEN).

Furthermore many countries require the reporting of cryptocurrency holdings and transactions on tax returns. This includes disclosing the acquisition sale or exchange of cryptocurrency and providing detailed information such as transaction dates amounts and counterparties involved.

It's crucial to keep accurate records of cryptocurrency transactions to comply with reporting requirements. This entails documenting the date amount purpose and parties involved in each transaction. Failure to report cryptocurrency transactions or providing inaccurate information can result in penalties fines or even legal consequences.

12.3 AML/KYC Regulations:

Anti-Money Laundering (AML) and Know Your Customer (KYC) regulations are designed to prevent and detect illicit activities such as money laundering terrorist financing or other criminal activities in the cryptocurrency space. AML/KYC regulations aim to ensure that cryptocurrency exchanges and financial institutions adopt robust practices to verify the identity of their customers and detect suspicious transactions.

KYC procedures require individuals to provide identification documents and other personal information when opening an account with a cryptocurrency exchange or trading platform. This information is used to verify the identity of the customer and ensure compliance with AML regulations.

For example to open an account on a cryptocurrency exchange you may be required to submit a copy of your passport or driver's license a proof of address document and possibly even a selfie or other biometric data for identity verification.

AML regulations require cryptocurrency exchanges to implement comprehensive systems for monitoring and reporting suspicious transactions. This includes implementing transaction monitoring tools establishing customer due diligence processes and reporting any suspicious activities to the relevant authorities.

12.4 Legal Implications of Crypto Ownership:

Owning cryptocurrency has legal implications that individuals should be aware of. While the legal status of cryptocurrency varies across jurisdictions understanding the potential legal consequences can help individuals make informed decisions and ensure compliance with applicable laws.

One legal implication is the potential for regulatory changes or restrictions on cryptocurrency ownership. Governments have been implementing regulations to address the risks associated with cryptocurrencies such as fraud market manipulation and tax evasion. These regulations may impact the legality and use of cryptocurrencies in certain jurisdictions.

For example some countries have banned or restricted the use of cryptocurrencies altogether while others have implemented licensing requirements for cryptocurrency businesses. It's essential for individuals to stay up-to-date with the legal landscape to understand the implications of owning and using cryptocurrencies.

Another legal consideration is the responsibility to protect private keys and wallets. Cryptocurrencies are stored in digital wallets and the private keys associated with these wallets are crucial for accessing and transferring the funds. Losing or compromising these private keys can result in the permanent loss of funds. Therefore individuals need to take appropriate measures to secure their private keys and wallets such as using strong passwords enabling two-factor authentication and utilizing hardware wallets.

Furthermore legal implications may arise when engaging in cryptocurrency-related activities such as Initial Coin Offerings (ICOs) or token sales. ICOs involve the issuance of digital tokens to raise funds for a project or venture. However the legal status of ICOs varies across jurisdictions and regulatory authorities have raised concerns regarding investor protection and fraud. Individuals participating in ICOs should carefully consider the legal implications and seek professional advice if necessary.

12.5 Government Enforcement Actions:

Government enforcement actions in the cryptocurrency space have been on the rise as regulators aim to protect investors maintain market integrity and combat illegal activities. These enforcement actions can take various forms such as investigations prosecutions and penalties.

One notable area of enforcement is fraudulent and unregistered Initial Coin Offerings (ICOs). Regulators have cracked down on ICOs that deceive investors with false promises or fail to comply with securities laws. For example the Securities and Exchange Commission (SEC) in the United States has taken legal action against numerous ICOs for selling unregistered securities or engaging in fraudulent practices.

Moreover cryptocurrency exchanges and trading platforms have faced regulatory scrutiny and enforcement actions. Cases of market manipulation inadequate security measures and failure to implement AML/KYC procedures have resulted in penalties fines and in some cases shutdowns of exchanges.

For instance the Financial Conduct Authority (FCA) in the United Kingdom has imposed strict requirements on cryptocurrency exchanges to address anti-money laundering and consumer protection concerns. Failure to comply with these requirements can result in regulatory action including fines and the suspension of operations.

Additionally governments have been cooperating internationally to combat illegal activities facilitated by cryptocurrencies. Authorities have combined efforts to track and trace transactions involved in money laundering terrorist financing and other criminal activities. This collaboration has resulted in multinational enforcement actions and the shutdown of illicit activities facilitated by cryptocurrencies.

In conclusion legal and regulatory compliance is a crucial aspect of dealing with cryptocurrencies. Taxation reporting requirements AML/KYC regulations legal implications of ownership and government enforcement actions are key areas that individuals and businesses need to understand and adhere to. Staying informed about the legal landscape and seeking professional advice when necessary will help ensure compliance and navigate the evolving regulatory environment in the cryptocurrency space.

V

Part 5: Using Bitcoin in Everyday Life

Using Bitcoin in everyday life is still relatively limited due to its volatility and limited merchant adoption, but it can serve as a store of value and a means for borderless transactions in certain contexts.

13

Everyday Uses of Bitcoin

13. Everyday Uses of Bitcoin

Bitcoin the pioneering cryptocurrency has gained significant popularity and adoption since its inception in 2009. While initially seen as a purely speculative investment Bitcoin has evolved to become a viable means of exchange. Today Bitcoin is being used in various everyday activities both online and offline. In this article we will delve into the different ways individuals can use Bitcoin in their everyday lives along with several examples.

13.1 Online and Retail Purchases

One of the most common uses of Bitcoin is for online and retail purchases. With the growing acceptance of Bitcoin by merchants worldwide consumers can use their Bitcoin holdings to shop for a wide range of products and services.

Many e-commerce platforms and retail stores have integrated

Bitcoin payment gateways allowing customers to make purchases using the cryptocurrency. For example Overstock.com a popular online retailer was one of the first major companies to adopt Bitcoin as a payment option.

Additionally numerous online marketplaces such as Bitify and OpenBazaar provide platforms for individuals to buy and sell products using Bitcoin as the primary currency. These platforms expand the use of Bitcoin beyond traditional retail channels and enable peer-to-peer transactions.

13.2 Gift Cards and Gift Services

Gift cards have long been a popular choice for birthdays holidays and special occasions. Bitcoin has now entered the world of gift-giving with the emergence of Bitcoin gift cards or vouchers. These gift cards function similarly to traditional gift cards but instead of being denominated in fiat currencies they hold a specific amount of Bitcoin. Recipients can then redeem the gift card and convert the Bitcoin into their preferred currency or use it for online purchases.

Several companies such as Gyft and eGifter offer Bitcoin gift cards that can be used at various retailers including Amazon Walmart and Starbucks. This provides a convenient way for individuals to introduce their friends and family to Bitcoin while giving them the flexibility to choose their own gifts.

Furthermore gift services specifically geared toward Bitcoin enthusiasts have emerged. These services allow users to send Bitcoin directly to someone's email address or mobile number as a gift. The recipient can then claim the Bitcoin and either store it or use it for transactions. This method reduces the complexity of Bitcoin transactions and makes it more accessible to non-technical users.

13.3 Peer-to-Peer Transactions

Bitcoin's decentralized nature makes it ideal for peer-to-peer transactions cutting out the need for intermediaries such as banks or payment processors. Peer-to-peer transactions involve directly transferring Bitcoin from one person to another without the need for a third-party authorization.

Platforms like LocalBitcoins and Paxful facilitate peer-to-peer Bitcoin exchanges. These platforms connect Bitcoin buyers and sellers allowing them to negotiate and complete transactions in a safe and secure manner. P2P exchanges provide individuals with greater control over their funds and allow for faster and cheaper transactions compared to traditional banking systems.

In addition to P2P exchanges there are also decentralized marketplaces that enable individuals to buy and sell goods and services directly with Bitcoin. One such example is OpenBazaar which functions as a decentralized marketplace powered by blockchain technology. Users can create online stores list items for sale and accept Bitcoin as payment.

13.4 Donations and Crowdfunding

Bitcoin has also found a home in the realm of charitable donations and crowdfunding. The transparency and traceability of

Bitcoin transactions make it an attractive option for donors as they can verify that their contributions are being used for the intended purpose.

Non-profit organizations and charities worldwide accept Bitcoin donations. By adding Bitcoin as a payment option these organizations can expand their reach and tap into a tech-savvy donor base. Some well-known organizations that accept Bitcoin donations include the Electronic Frontier Foundation (EFF WikiLeaks and the Water Project.

Furthermore crowdfunding platforms have started to embrace Bitcoin. Platforms like Kickstarter and Indiegogo have integrated Bitcoin payment options providing entrepreneurs and creative individuals with an alternative funding method. Bitcoin's global nature also allows for cross-border crowdfunding campaigns enabling donors from anywhere in the world to contribute.

13.5 Remittances and Cross-Border Payments

Bitcoin has the potential to revolutionize international remittances and cross-border payments. Traditional remittance services are often expensive time-consuming and subject to various restrictions and regulations. Bitcoin offers a borderless and efficient alternative.

By leveraging Bitcoin individuals can send money internationally with reduced fees and faster transaction times. This is particularly beneficial for people in developing countries who rely on remittances from family members working abroad.

For example the BitPesa platform allows users in Africa to send money to Kenya Nigeria Uganda and Tanzania using Bitcoin. BitPesa converts the sent Bitcoin local recipient need the. for Bitcoin become into enabling to activities the cryptocurrency. Whether it be for online purchases gift cards peer-to-peer transactions donations or cross-border payments Bitcoin offers a range of benefits such as low fees increased security and borderless transactions. As adoption continues to grow and more companies and individuals embrace Bitcoin its everyday use will likely expand further.

14

Bitcoin and Privacy

Maintaining privacy while using Bitcoin is a nuanced aspect, influenced by various factors. First and foremost, understanding that Bitcoin transactions are stored on a public ledger, the blockchain, is essential. To enhance privacy, users can employ techniques like CoinJoin or utilize privacy-focused cryptocurrencies such as Monero or Zcash, which offer more advanced privacy features. Wallet choice is critical; opting for wallets that prioritize privacy and allow you to control your private keys can offer better anonymity. Additionally, avoiding the reuse of Bitcoin addresses and frequently generating new addresses can help protect your identity. Being cautious about revealing personal information and practicing good cybersecurity hygiene is also crucial to safeguard your privacy in the Bitcoin ecosystem. Lastly, staying informed about evolving privacy solutions and potential vulnerabilities is vital to maintain anonymity while using Bitcoin.

14.1 Privacy Coins

Bitcoin the first and most well-known cryptocurrency has often been touted as a secure and anonymous form of digital payment. However it is essential to understand that Bitcoin's underlying technology blockchain is designed to be transparent and immutable. While Bitcoin addresses are pseudonymous meaning they do not directly reveal the identity of the user all transactions made with Bitcoin are recorded on a public ledger known as the blockchain. This means that anyone can view the transaction details such as the amount sent and the sending and receiving addresses.

To address the need for financial privacy privacy coins were introduced. These cryptocurrencies aim to provide enhanced privacy and anonymity features that go beyond Bitcoin's transparent nature. Privacy coins achieve this by implementing various privacy-focused techniques such as ring signatures stealth addresses and confidential transactions.

One example of a privacy coin is Monero (XMR). Monero uses ring signatures which mix the spender's transaction with a group of other transactions to make it difficult to determine the exact source of the funds. It also employs stealth addresses to obfuscate the recipient's identity. Additionally Monero hides the amount of each transaction using confidential transactions ensuring that the transaction value remains private.

Another privacy coin is Zcash (ZEC which utilizes a technology called zero-knowledge proofs. Zero-knowledge proofs allow for the verification of transactions without revealing any information about the sender receiver or transaction amount. This enables secure and anonymous transactions while still maintaining the decentralization and security properties of blockchain technology.

14.2 Anonymity vs Transparency

The debate around privacy and transparency revolves around striking a balance between protecting individual privacy rights and ensuring security and accountability in the financial system. While privacy coins offer enhanced privacy features they also raise concerns about their potential misuse for illicit activities such as money laundering and funding criminal enterprises.

Proponents of privacy coins argue that privacy is a fundamental human right and individuals should have the right to control the disclosure of their financial transactions. They believe that increased financial privacy can protect individuals from surveillance identity theft and profiling.

On the other hand regulators and law enforcement agencies express concerns that privacy coins could enable illicit activities and hinder the ability to trace and investigate criminal transactions. They argue that transparency is crucial for maintaining the integrity of the financial system and combating money laundering terrorist financing and other illicit activities.

Striking a balance between privacy and transparency is a complex task. It requires considering both the individual's right to privacy and the need for regulatory oversight and law enforcement. Technological advancements such as privacy coins challenge existing regulatory frameworks and force policymakers to adapt to the changing landscape of digital currencies.

14.3 Privacy Concerns and Solutions

While privacy coins offer enhanced privacy features there are still potential privacy concerns that users should be aware of. Here are some privacy concerns and potential solutions:

1. Address Reuse: Reusing the same address for multiple transactions can compromise privacy. It allows anyone to link the transactions made to the same address potentially revealing a user's spending patterns. To address this concern users should employ best practices and generate a new address for each transaction.

2. Network Analysis: Sophisticated network analysis techniques can be used to trace transactions and potentially identify the parties involved. Privacy coins address this concern by implementing techniques like ring signatures and zero-knowledge proofs which obfuscate transaction details and make it difficult to trace the origin and destination of funds.

3. Metadata Leaks: While privacy coins can hide transaction details other forms of metadata such as transaction timing and network traffic analysis can still be used to gain insights into users' activities. One solution to combat metadata leaks is by using privacy-enhancing technologies like Tor or VPNs to obfuscate network traffic and protect user anonymity.

4. Exchange and Third-Party Risks: Exchanges and third-party services can pose privacy risks by collecting and storing user data. Users should be cautious and choose reputable platforms that prioritize user privacy and implement strict data protection

measures.

14.4 Protecting Your Financial Privacy

Privacy is a multifaceted concept and protecting your financial privacy goes beyond using privacy coins. Here are some additional measures you can take to enhance your financial privacy:

1. Use Secure Wallets: Employ secure wallets to store your cryptocurrencies. Hardware wallets such as Ledger or Trezor provide an added layer of security by keeping your private keys offline and away from potential online threats.

2. Mixers or Tumblers: If you are using transparent cryptocurrencies like Bitcoin you can use mixers or tumblers to mix your coins with others making it harder to trace the flow of funds. These services pool transactions together to create a level of anonymity while preserving the fungibility of the currency.

3. Self-Custody: Consider self-custody options to maintain full control over your funds. This involves storing your cryptocurrencies in a wallet where you control the private keys reducing the risk of third-party data breaches.

4. Accessing Secure Networks: When transacting online ensure that you are connected to secure networks especially when dealing with sensitive financial transactions. Public Wi-Fi networks can be easily compromised potentially compromising your financial privacy.

5. Monitor Online Presence: Be mindful of the information

you share publicly online especially on social media platforms. Avoid exposing sensitive financial details that could be used to track or identify your transactions.

6. Privacy Education: Stay updated with the latest developments in privacy-enhancing technologies and best practices. Continually educating yourself about privacy tools and techniques can help you maintain control over your financial privacy.

14.5 Privacy in the Age of Surveillance

Financial privacy has become increasingly important in an age of widespread surveillance and data collection. Governments and corporations are continuously collecting vast amounts of personal data for various purposes including targeted advertising monitoring consumer behavior and law enforcement activities.

Cryptocurrencies and privacy coins offer a potential solution to mitigate some of the privacy concerns associated with traditional financial systems. However it is essential to recognize that financial privacy extends beyond the realm of cryptocurrencies. The broader issues of data privacy surveillance and online tracking need to be addressed holistically.

Regulatory frameworks should strike a balance between enabling privacy rights and ensuring that financial systems are not abused for illicit activities. This requires collaboration between policymakers technologists and privacy advocates to establish guidelines that protect individual privacy while maintaining the necessary safeguards against criminal activities.

As users it is critical to be conscious of our digital footprint and proactive in protecting our privacy. Adopting privacy-enhancing technologies using secure networks practicing data minimization and being aware of our rights as individuals can contribute to preserving financial privacy in the age of surveillance.

In conclusion privacy coins like Monero and Zcash offer enhanced privacy features that go beyond Bitcoin's transparency. They employ techniques like ring signatures stealth addresses and zero-knowledge proofs to mitigate privacy concerns. However financial privacy requires a multifaceted approach including best practices secure wallets and privacy education. Balancing privacy and transparency is an ongoing challenge necessitating collaboration between stakeholders to shape regulatory frameworks that protect individual privacy while addressing the need for oversight and security. It is crucial to understand that financial privacy extends beyond cryptocurrencies and encompasses broader issues of data privacy surveillance and online tracking.

VI

Part 6: Bitcoin and the Ecosystem

Bitcoin and the ecosystem surrounding it encompass a wide range of innovations, services, and communities, fostering a dynamic and rapidly evolving landscape in the world of cryptocurrencies.

15

Bitcoin's Impact on Finance and Economics

Bitcoin's impact on finance and economics is multifaceted, shaped by a complex interplay of factors. Firstly, it has introduced the concept of decentralized digital currencies and blockchain technology, challenging traditional financial systems and fostering innovation in areas like cross-border payments and smart contracts. Bitcoin's limited supply, often compared to gold, has sparked discussions about its potential role as a hedge against inflation and economic instability, influencing investment strategies and portfolio diversification.

However, its price volatility has raised concerns regarding its suitability as a stable store of value and medium of exchange. Moreover, regulatory developments and government responses have varied globally, impacting its adoption and legitimacy in different jurisdictions. Institutional interest, evidenced by investments from major corporations and asset managers, has both validated and impacted Bitcoin's role in the broader economy.

Furthermore, Bitcoin has given rise to a new asset class and financial ecosystem, including the emergence of cryptocurrency exchanges, lending platforms, and decentralized finance (DeFi) projects, contributing to the evolution of financial markets. It has also sparked discussions about central bank digital currencies (CBDCs) and their potential impact on monetary policy.

In conclusion, Bitcoin's influence on finance and economics is a complex and evolving phenomenon, with its role continually reshaping traditional financial paradigms, spurring innovation, and provoking regulatory and economic debates. Understanding and navigating this landscape requires a comprehensive perspective on its technological, economic, and regulatory aspects.

15.1 Disruptive Potential of Bitcoin

Bitcoin as a decentralized digital currency has the potential to disrupt the traditional financial systems in various ways. One of the key disruptive potentials is the elimination of intermediaries in financial transactions. By using a peer-to-peer network Bitcoin enables users to transact directly without the need for banks or other financial institutions. This peer-to-peer nature allows for faster and cheaper transactions reducing the costs associated with traditional financial systems.

Additionally Bitcoin's underlying technology the blockchain creates a transparent and immutable ledger of all transactions. This feature enhances trust between participants as they can easily verify transaction histories. It also reduces the possibility of fraud or manipulation.

Furthermore Bitcoin's limited supply and decentralized nature make it resistant to government control or manipulation. This means that Bitcoin can act as an alternative store of value potentially providing a hedge against inflation or economic instability.

15.2 Monetary Policy Implications

Bitcoin's limited supply and decentralized nature also have implications for monetary policy. Unlike traditional fiat currencies which can be easily created or manipulated by central banks Bitcoin operates on a fixed supply schedule. There will only ever be a maximum of 21 million bitcoins in circulation. This scarcity gives Bitcoin a deflationary nature where the value of the currency may increase over time.

This deflationary nature of Bitcoin challenges conventional monetary policy which aims to maintain a stable inflation rate. Central banks often use inflation targeting to stimulate economic growth or control inflation. However Bitcoin's fixed supply makes it immune to such policy measures potentially complicating economic management.

Moreover as Bitcoin gains wider acceptance it may pose challenges to the dominance of traditional fiat currencies. If people start using Bitcoin for everyday transactions central banks could lose their ability to control money supply and interest rates potentially impacting their ability to manage economic stability.

15.3 Financial Inclusion and Accessibility

Bitcoin has the potential to improve financial inclusion and accessibility especially for individuals who are unbanked or underbanked. In many parts of the world traditional banking services are limited expensive or inaccessible for various reasons. Bitcoin offers an alternative financial system that does not require a physical presence or lengthy verification processes.

With Bitcoin anyone with an internet connection can create a digital wallet and start transacting. This opens up opportunities for individuals in remote areas developing countries or regions with limited banking infrastructure to participate in the global economy. By enabling peer-to-peer transactions Bitcoin can facilitate cross-border remittances reducing the costs and time associated with traditional remittance methods.

Furthermore Bitcoin has the potential to provide financial services to those who have been excluded from the traditional banking system due to lack of identification or credit history. Through Bitcoin individuals can access basic financial services such as savings payments and loans without relying on traditional banking systems.

15.4 Challenges to Traditional Banking

The rise of Bitcoin poses several challenges to traditional banking systems. As more people adopt Bitcoin there may be a decline in demand for traditional banking services such as checking accounts or credit cards. Bitcoin's peer-to-peer transactions and lower transaction costs make it an attractive alternative for individuals seeking a more efficient and cost-effective way to manage their finances.

Moreover Bitcoin's decentralized nature challenges the centralized control exerted by banks. With Bitcoin individuals have full control over their funds and can transact directly with others. This reduces the need for intermediaries potentially reducing the revenue generated by banks from transaction fees.

Furthermore traditional banks may face competition from Bitcoin-related financial services such as bitcoin exchanges wallets and lending platforms. These services offer alternatives to traditional banking services and may attract customers seeking the benefits of the Bitcoin ecosystem.

However it is important to note that Bitcoin and traditional banking systems are not mutually exclusive. Many financial institutions are starting to explore the integration of Bitcoin and blockchain technology into their existing operations. This can lead to collaborations between traditional banks and Bitcoin-related businesses creating a hybrid financial ecosystem that combines the strengths of both systems.

In conclusion Bitcoin has the potential to disrupt the traditional finance and economics landscape in significant ways. Its peer-to-peer nature transparency and limited supply make it an attractive alternative to traditional financial systems. Bitcoin's impact can be observed in financial inclusion monetary policy implications and the challenges it poses to traditional banking. It is crucial to monitor the ongoing developments in the Bitcoin ecosystem as it continues to shape the future of finance and economics.

16

Environmental and Energy Considerations

Environmental and energy considerations are increasingly important in the context of Bitcoin mining and cryptocurrency operations. Bitcoin's energy-intensive proof-of-work (PoW) consensus mechanism has raised concerns about its carbon footprint and sustainability. The environmental impact of mining, primarily fueled by coal-powered plants in some regions, has prompted discussions about its contribution to greenhouse gas emissions.

Efforts to mitigate these concerns include a shift toward renewable energy sources for mining operations, with some large-scale miners establishing facilities near renewable energy hubs. Additionally, alternative consensus mechanisms like proof-of-stake (PoS) are gaining attention for their lower energy requirements. Striking a balance between cryptocurrency innovation and environmental sustainability remains a pressing challenge, with ongoing debates and initiatives to reduce the carbon footprint of the crypto industry.

16.1 Bitcoin Mining and Energy Consumption

Bitcoin mining is the process of validating and adding new transactions to the blockchain the decentralized ledger that records all Bitcoin transactions. It is achieved through massive computational power solving complex mathematical problems and competing with other miners in a race to find the solution. This process requires a significant amount of energy consumption.

The energy consumption of Bitcoin mining has been a topic of concern and debate. The decentralized nature of Bitcoin mining means that anyone with access to powerful hardware can participate in the mining process. As a result miners have increased the computational power dedicated to mining to stay competitive leading to a rise in energy consumption.

The energy consumption of Bitcoin mining can be attributed to two main factors. First the hardware used for mining especially ASIC (Application-Specific Integrated Circuit) miners requires a significant amount of electricity to operate. These machines are designed specifically for mining and are highly efficient at performing the necessary calculations. However their efficiency comes at the cost of increased power consumption.

The second factor contributing to the energy consumption is the consensus algorithm used by Bitcoin known as proof-of-work. This algorithm ensures that the network reaches a consensus on the validity of transactions by requiring miners to provide proof of their computational work. This process is energy-intensive as it involves continuously running the mining hardware and

107

solving complex mathematical problems.

The energy consumption of Bitcoin mining has attracted criticism as it contributes to carbon emissions and puts pressure on global energy resources. In 2019 a report estimated that Bitcoin mining alone accounted for 0.22% of the world's total electricity consumption surpassing the energy consumption of many countries.

16.2 Sustainable Mining Practices

To address the environmental concerns associated with Bitcoin mining there have been efforts to promote sustainable mining practices. These practices aim to reduce the carbon footprint of mining operations and make the process more environmentally friendly.

One approach to sustainable mining is the use of renewable energy sources. By utilizing renewable energy such as solar wind or hydroelectric power miners can reduce their reliance on fossil fuels and decrease carbon emissions. Several mining farms and operations have started adopting renewable energy solutions either through on-site installations or by purchasing renewable energy credits.

Another strategy is the optimization of mining hardware and infrastructure. More energy-efficient ASIC miners are being developed which help reduce energy consumption while maintaining the necessary computational power for mining. Additionally mining facilities can implement energy-saving measures such as efficient cooling systems and proper insulation to minimize energy waste.

Furthermore some mining operations are exploring the concept of co-location where multiple businesses share the same infrastructure and resources. This approach can maximize energy efficiency by reducing redundancies and optimizing resource utilization.

16.3 Renewable Energy Solutions

Renewable energy solutions play a crucial role in making Bitcoin mining more environmentally sustainable. By harnessing the power of natural resources miners can reduce their carbon footprint and contribute to a cleaner energy future.

Solar energy is one of the most promising renewable energy sources for Bitcoin mining. Solar panels can be installed on mining facilities' rooftops or in nearby areas to generate electricity. Mining farms located in regions with abundant sunlight such as the southwestern parts of the United States have embraced solar energy solutions. They can directly power their mining operations or supplement their electricity needs with solar power.

Wind energy is another renewable option for powering mining operations. Wind turbines can be installed in windy regions such as coastal areas or open plains to generate electricity. Miners can either establish their wind farms or partner with existing wind energy projects. Many countries like Denmark and Germany have invested heavily in wind energy infrastructure making it an attractive option for sustainable mining practices.

Hydroelectric power is also well-suited for Bitcoin mining. Hydroelectric dams and power stations generate electricity by harnessing the force of flowing water. Regions with abundant water resources and suitable topography can integrate mining operations with hydroelectric power plants. This approach not only provides renewable energy but also helps to balance seasonal fluctuations in electricity demand.

16.4 Environmental Criticisms and Debates

Despite the efforts to promote sustainable mining practices Bitcoin mining continues to face environmental criticisms and debates. Here are some key points of contention:

1. Carbon Footprint: Critics argue that Bitcoin mining's high energy consumption contributes to carbon emissions and exacerbates climate change. They claim that the energy consumption of Bitcoin mining is wasteful and unnecessary.

2. E-Waste: The rapid advancement of mining technology leads to the constant upgrade and replacement of mining hardware. The discarded hardware results in electronic waste (e-waste which poses environmental risks when not properly managed or recycled.

3. Centralization Concerns: Some argue that Bitcoin mining is becoming increasingly centralized with a few major mining pools dominating the network. This concentration of power can lead to environmental concerns as more power is concentrated in the hands of a few entities potentially impacting decision-making processes related to sustainability.

4. Energy Grid Strain: Critics suggest that the increased demand for energy due to Bitcoin mining can strain local energy grids especially in regions with limited electricity supply. This strain on the energy infrastructure can have adverse effects on the environment and the local community.

5. Indirect Environmental Impact: Bitcoin mining requires the manufacture and transport of mining hardware which adds to the overall environmental impact. The extraction of raw materials such as rare metals used in the production of mining hardware can also have negative environmental consequences.

16.5 The Path to Eco-Friendly Cryptocurrency

To overcome the environmental challenges associated with Bitcoin mining various initiatives and solutions are being explored. These efforts aim to make cryptocurrency mining more sustainable and reduce its impact on the environment.

1. Transition to Proof-of-Stake: One proposed solution is transitioning from the energy-intensive proof-of-work consensus algorithm to the proof-of-stake algorithm. Unlike proof-of-work proof-of-stake does not require miners to solve complex mathematical problems but instead selects validators based on the number of cryptocurrency units they hold. This approach significantly reduces energy consumption making mining more eco-friendly.

2. Energy Offsetting: Some mining operations are actively working on offsetting their carbon emissions by investing in carbon offset projects. By supporting initiatives that reduce

greenhouse gas emissions or promote renewable energy miners can compensate for the environmental impact of their operations.

3. Green Mining Index: The development of a green mining index or certification system can incentivize sustainable practices within the mining industry. This index would evaluate mining operations based on their use of renewable energy energy efficiency and other environmentally friendly criteria. Miners with higher scores would be recognized and rewarded encouraging the adoption of more sustainable practices.

4. Community Engagement: Engaging local communities and stakeholders is crucial for creating sustainable mining practices. Miners can collaborate with environmental organizations community leaders and regulatory bodies to address concerns implement best practices and ensure transparency in their operations.

5. Education and Awareness: Increasing public awareness about the environmental impact of Bitcoin mining can drive demand for eco-friendly cryptocurrencies and push the industry to adopt sustainable practices. Efforts to educate the public about the benefits of renewable energy and the potential of blockchain technology in supporting clean energy initiatives can help create a more environmentally conscious mining industry.

In conclusion Bitcoin mining's energy consumption has sparked concerns about its environmental impact. However there are ongoing efforts to promote sustainable mining practices such as leveraging renewable energy sources and optimizing mining hardware and infrastructure. Additionally the cryptocurrency industry is exploring alternative consensus algorithms engaging in carbon offsetting and aiming for community participation to reduce the ecological footprint of mining operations. These initiatives along with increased awareness and education will play a vital role in shaping the future of eco-friendly cryptocurrency.

VII

Part 7: Advanced Topics in Bitcoin

Advanced topics in Bitcoin delve into intricate subjects such as layer two solutions, smart contracts, privacy enhancements, and governance models, shaping the future of the cryptocurrency.

17

Smart Contracts and Bitcoin

17. Smart Contracts and Bitcoin

Smart contracts are self-executing contracts with the terms of the agreement directly written into lines of code. These contracts automatically execute when the predetermined conditions specified in the code are satisfied. While smart contracts are often associated with the Ethereum blockchain Bitcoin also supports a limited form of smart contracts through its scripting language.

17.1 Bitcoin Scripting Language

Bitcoin's scripting language is a simple stack-based programming language that allows users to define conditions under which funds can be spent. Instead of writing complex programs Bitcoin's scripting language is intentionally limited and designed to be secure to prevent potential vulnerabilities.

Bitcoin's scripting language allows users to create several

commonly used types of transactions including multi-signature transactions time-locked transactions and atomic swaps. These features provide increased security and flexibility to Bitcoin users.

Let's take a closer look at some of the use cases for smart contracts in Bitcoin.

17.2 Use Cases for Bitcoin Smart Contracts

a) Multi-Signature Transactions: Bitcoin's scripting language allows for the creation of multi-signature transactions where more than one signature is required to spend the funds. This can be particularly useful for organizations or joint accounts where multiple parties need to approve transactions. For example a company could create a 2-of-3 multi-signature address requiring any two out of three authorized parties to sign off on transactions.

b) Time-Locked Transactions: Bitcoin also supports time-locked transactions where funds are locked and cannot be spent until a specified future time or block height. Time-locked transactions can be useful in various scenarios such as ensuring delayed access to funds creating time-bound escrow services or implementing conditional payments. For instance a merchant might require that a customer's payment is locked in a time-locked transaction for a specified period before the funds are released.

c) Atomic Swaps: Another use case for Bitcoin smart contracts is atomic swaps which allow for the exchange of one cryptocurrency for another directly between different blockchain networks without the need for intermediaries. Atomic swaps are achieved through smart contracts that ensure both parties involved in the swap receive their desired cryptocurrencies simultaneously reducing the need for trust and minimizing counterparty risk.

While Bitcoin's scripting language provides some smart contract functionality it is important to note that it is less expressive and more limited compared to platforms like Ethereum.

17.3 Comparison with Ethereum and Other Platforms

Ethereum is widely regarded as the leading platform for smart contracts due to its more expressive and Turing-complete programming language Solidity. Solidity allows developers to create highly complex smart contracts with intricate logic and functionality. Ethereum's smart contracts can interact with each other enabling the creation of decentralized applications (DApps) on the Ethereum blockchain.

In contrast Bitcoin's script language is a minimalist language that lacks the ability to create more sophisticated smart contracts. Bitcoin's scripting language was intentionally designed to prioritize security and simplicity over versatility. This design choice reduces the risk of potential bugs and vulnerabilities but limits the potential use cases for smart contracts on the Bitcoin network.

Other blockchain platforms such as EOS NEO and Cardano also offer their own smart contract functionalities with varying levels of complexity and features. These platforms aim to address some of the limitations faced by Bitcoin and Ethereum by offering more scalability interoperability and developer-friendly environments.

17.4 Limitations and Challenges

While Bitcoin's limited smart contract functionality may be suitable for certain use cases it poses limitations compared to more sophisticated platforms like Ethereum. Some of the challenges and limitations of Bitcoin's smart contract implementation include:

a) Limited Expressivity: Bitcoin's scripting language lacks the ability to create complex logic loops and conditional statements making it challenging to implement advanced smart contract functionalities.

b) Cost and Speed: Bitcoin's scripting language can be less efficient in terms of cost and speed compared to other platforms. The limited design of Bitcoin's scripting language requires more operations to accomplish certain tasks resulting in higher transaction fees and longer confirmation times.

c) Upgradability: Unlike Ethereum Bitcoin lacks a built-in mechanism for smart contract upgradability. Once a script is deployed on the Bitcoin network it cannot be modified or improved without creating a new transaction and potentially affecting all previous transactions relying on that script.

d) Scalability: Bitcoin's scalability challenges also affect smart contracts. The limited block size and transaction throughput of the Bitcoin network can lead to congestion and delays in executing smart contracts.

Despite these limitations Bitcoin's simplicity and robustness have made it a reliable platform for financial transactions and its limited smart contract capabilities can still cater to a range of use cases in a secure manner.

Conclusion

While Bitcoin's primary focus is on providing a decentralized peer-to-peer electronic cash system it also offers some smart contract capabilities through its scripting language. These smart contracts allow for the creation of multi-signature transactions time-locked transactions and atomic swaps providing increased security and flexibility to Bitcoin users.

However it's important to acknowledge that Bitcoin's smart contract functionality is limited compared to platforms like Ethereum. Ethereum's Turing-complete programming language allows for the creation of more complex and sophisticated smart contracts enabling the development of DApps and more advanced decentralized systems.

Nevertheless Bitcoin's minimalist design prioritizes security and simplicity making it a robust and reliable platform for financial transactions. While its smart contract capabilities might not be as extensive as some other platforms Bitcoin's focus on transactional security has contributed to its enduring popularity and relevance in the crypto space.

18

Bitcoin Development and Open Source

Bitcoin development and open-source principles are closely intertwined, shaping the evolution of the cryptocurrency. Bitcoin's source code is open to the public, allowing anyone to view, modify, or propose changes to the protocol. This transparency fosters a collaborative and decentralized approach to development, with a global community of developers, known as the Bitcoin Core team, continuously working on improvements and security enhancements.

18.1 Bitcoin Core and Protocol Development

Bitcoin is a decentralized cryptocurrency that operates on a peer-to-peer network. The development of Bitcoin is led by a group of dedicated developers who work on improving the Bitcoin Core software. Bitcoin Core is the reference implementation of the Bitcoin protocol and acts as the backbone of the entire Bitcoin network.

The development of Bitcoin Core involves a wide range of

tasks including bug fixes performance improvements security enhancements and the implementation of new features. Developers contribute to the project by reviewing code proposing and implementing changes and engaging in discussions with the community to ensure the stability security and decentralization of the Bitcoin network.

One of the key principles of Bitcoin development is open source collaboration which means that anyone can view modify and share the source code of Bitcoin Core. This open approach fosters transparency trust and innovation by allowing developers from all over the world to contribute to the development of Bitcoin. It also enables peer review allowing bugs and vulnerabilities to be identified and fixed more rapidly.

The development of Bitcoin Core is primarily driven by the Bitcoin Core development team which consists of a core group of maintainers and contributors. However the development process is open to anyone who wants to contribute and there are several ways for developers to get involved such as submitting bug reports proposing and implementing improvements and participating in the code review process.

18.2 Contributions to the Bitcoin Ecosystem

Bitcoin's open source nature has led to the creation of a vast ecosystem of projects and applications built on top of the Bitcoin protocol. These projects span a wide range of industries and use cases including wallets exchanges payment processors decentralized applications (dApps and more.

Open source development has played a crucial role in the growth and adoption of Bitcoin. It has allowed developers to leverage the work of others and build upon existing software reducing the time and effort required to develop new applications. This has led to an increase in innovation and the development of diverse and powerful tools and services that make using Bitcoin more accessible and secure.

For example Bitcoin wallets are software applications that allow users to manage their Bitcoin holdings. There are numerous Bitcoin wallet projects available both on mobile and desktop platforms that offer different features and levels of security. These wallets are often open source allowing users to verify the code and trust that their funds are stored securely.

Another example is the Lightning Network a Layer 2 scaling solution for Bitcoin. It uses smart contracts to enable fast and low-cost off-chain transactions. The Lightning Network is an open source project that has been developed by multiple teams and individuals contributing to its widespread adoption and continuous improvement.

Open source development also encourages collaboration and knowledge-sharing within the Bitcoin community. Developers can collaborate with each other share ideas and learn from each other's work. This collaborative environment has led to the formation of Bitcoin developer communities where developers come together to discuss and work on various Bitcoin-related projects such as Bitcoin Improvement Proposals (BIPs) and research papers.

18.3 Forks and Updates

Bitcoin's open source nature also allows for the possibility of forks and updates to the protocol. A fork occurs when there is a divergence in the Bitcoin network resulting in two separate blockchains with different rules. This can happen due to disagreements within the community or to implement new features improvements or fixes to the protocol.

There have been several notable forks of Bitcoin such as Bitcoin Cash (BCH) and Bitcoin SV (BSV which were created to increase the block size limit and improve scalability. These forks aimed to address the scalability issues associated with Bitcoin's limited transaction capacity.

Forks can be contentious leading to debates and disagreements within the community. However they can also be an opportunity for innovation and experimentation. Forks allow developers to test new ideas implement changes more rapidly and explore alternative approaches to improve the Bitcoin protocol.

Updates to the Bitcoin protocol are proposed and implemented through the Bitcoin Improvement Proposal (BIP) process. BIPs are design documents that outline new features improvements or changes to the Bitcoin protocol. Developers and community members can submit BIPs for discussion and review and if accepted they can be implemented into the Bitcoin codebase.

Updates to the protocol can improve various aspects of the Bitcoin network such as scalability privacy security and functionality. These updates are crucial to ensuring that Bitcoin remains a robust and secure decentralized digital currency.

18.4 Community Involvement

Community involvement is essential for the development and growth of Bitcoin. The Bitcoin community consists of developers users miners businesses and enthusiasts who actively engage in discussions contribute to projects and promote the adoption of Bitcoin.

One way the community gets involved is through Bitcoin meetups and conferences. These events provide a platform for developers and enthusiasts to network share ideas and collaborate on Bitcoin-related projects. They also serve as an opportunity to educate newcomers and raise awareness about Bitcoin and its underlying technology.

The Bitcoin community also actively engages in online forums and discussion boards. Platforms like BitcoinTalk and Reddit are popular among community members who discuss various aspects of Bitcoin ask questions and share their knowledge and experiences. These online communities provide a space for developers to interact with users and receive feedback on their work.

Additionally the community supports the development of Bitcoin through financial contributions. Bitcoin developers often rely on donations from the community to fund their work. Many developers have set up donation addresses or crowdfunding campaigns to receive support from the community.

The involvement of the community in the development process plays a vital role in ensuring that the Bitcoin protocol remains decentralized and resistant to external influences. It allows for a diverse range of perspectives and ideas to be considered and contributes to the long-term sustainability of the Bitcoin network.

18.5 Building on the Bitcoin Blockchain

The open source nature of Bitcoin also allows developers to build on top of the Bitcoin blockchain creating new applications platforms and services that leverage the security and decentralization of the Bitcoin network.

One notable example is the development of decentralized finance (DeFi) applications on the Bitcoin blockchain. DeFi refers to the use of blockchain technology and cryptocurrencies to recreate traditional financial instruments such as lending borrowing and trading in a decentralized and trustless manner. Several projects have emerged that enable decentralized lending and borrowing on the Bitcoin blockchain allowing users to earn interest on their Bitcoin holdings or access loans without relying on traditional financial institutions.

Another example is the integration of smart contracts on the Bitcoin blockchain. While Bitcoin's native scripting language is limited compared to other blockchain platforms like Ethereum developers have found ways to enable smart contract functionality on the Bitcoin blockchain. Projects like Rootstock (RSK) and Liquid Network have introduced sidechains that are compatible with Bitcoin allowing developers to build and deploy smart contracts that interact with Bitcoin assets.

Furthermore open source projects have facilitated the development of Bitcoin wallets exchanges payment processors and other tools and services that make it easier for users to interact with Bitcoin. These projects provide a range of features including user-friendly interfaces secure storage and seamless integration with existing financial systems.

Building on the Bitcoin blockchain allows developers to leverage the security and decentralization of the Bitcoin network while providing users with new and innovative ways to interact with Bitcoin. It fosters a vibrant ecosystem of applications that enhance the usability functionality and adoption of Bitcoin.

In conclusion the open source nature of Bitcoin has been instrumental in its development and growth. The Bitcoin community comprising developers users miners businesses and enthusiasts actively contributes to the development of Bitcoin Core and the protocol. Open source collaboration enables innovation transparency and trust within the Bitcoin ecosystem. It has led to the creation of diverse projects and applications built on top of the Bitcoin blockchain such as wallets exchanges payment processors DeFi platforms and more. Forks and updates to the Bitcoin protocol ensure its scalability security and functionality. Community involvement and financial support play a vital role in sustaining the development of Bitcoin. Overall open source development and community involvement have been instrumental in making Bitcoin a decentralized and widely adopted cryptocurrency.

19

Bitcoin in a Global Context

Bitcoin holds a unique position in a global context as a decentralized digital currency. It transcends traditional borders, enabling
cross-border transactions and financial inclusion for individuals worldwide. Its role as a global store of value is increasingly
recognized, with some considering it a hedge against economic
uncertainty and inflation. However, regulatory approaches and
acceptance of Bitcoin vary widely among countries, presenting
a complex landscape for its adoption and use. The global Bitcoin
community continues to advocate for its potential to reshape
the global financial system while navigating diverse regulatory
and cultural perspectives on its role in the global economy.

19.1 Bitcoin Adoption Around the World

Bitcoin a decentralized digital currency has gained significant
traction around the world since its inception in 2009. The
adoption of Bitcoin varies across different countries and regions
with some embracing it as a new form of payment and store
of value while others are cautious or even hostile towards its
integration into mainstream financial systems.

One of the key factors driving Bitcoin adoption is economic instability. In countries experiencing high inflation rates or strict capital controls individuals may turn to Bitcoin as a hedge against depreciation or as a means to bypass restrictions on transferring money abroad. Venezuela for example has seen a surge in Bitcoin adoption in recent years due to its hyperinflationary economic crisis. Bitcoin provides Venezuelans with a secure storage of value and a means of conducting international transactions.

Another driver of Bitcoin adoption is the desire for financial inclusivity. In countries with underdeveloped banking systems or a large unbanked population Bitcoin can offer an alternative means of accessing financial services. For example in Africa where a significant portion of the population lacks access to traditional banking Bitcoin is being used as a medium of exchange and a store of value. Mobile-based platforms like BitPesa in Kenya facilitate Bitcoin transactions and provide financial services to the unbanked.

Furthermore geopolitical factors can influence Bitcoin adoption. In countries facing economic sanctions or political turmoil Bitcoin can help individuals circumvent financial restrictions and maintain access to global markets. Iran for example has witnessed a surge in Bitcoin mining and trading following US-imposed sanctions allowing Iranians to continue engaging in international trade.

19.2 Geopolitical Implications

The decentralized nature of Bitcoin poses challenges and opportunities on a global scale. Governments and central banks have different approaches to Bitcoin regulation ranging from embracing it as a legal form of payment to outright bans. This leads to geopolitical implications that can impact global financial systems and diplomatic relationships.

When countries embrace Bitcoin they can benefit from increased innovation and investment in the blockchain technology that underlies it. Nations that are forward-thinking in their approach to cryptocurrency regulation can attract blockchain startups and foster technological advancements. This can give them a competitive advantage in the digital economy and stimulate economic growth.

On the other hand governments that view Bitcoin as a threat to their monetary sovereignty may seek to restrict or ban its use. China for example has imposed strict regulations on Bitcoin exchanges and initial coin offerings (ICOs) to limit capital outflows and control the flow of digital assets. Such actions can inhibit the development of the cryptocurrency industry in those countries potentially stifling innovation and driving talent and capital elsewhere.

In addition to the direct impact on individual countries the global adoption of Bitcoin can also influence international relations. As Bitcoin transactions are borderless and don't rely on traditional financial intermediaries they can be used for cross-border payments and remittances bypassing traditional banking systems. This can complicate regulatory efforts and potentially undermine the influence of central banks.

19.3 Cross-Border Trade and Remittances

Bitcoin has the potential to revolutionize cross-border trade and remittances by providing a fast and low-cost alternative to traditional payment systems. Traditional methods such as wire transfers and international money transfer operators (MTOs are often slow expensive and subject to complex regulatory requirements.

Bitcoin enables individuals and businesses to send and receive funds directly without the need for intermediaries. This can significantly reduce transaction fees and friction associated with cross-border payments. Moreover the speed of Bitcoin transactions can be advantageous for international trade as it eliminates the delays associated with bank transfers.

Countries with high remittance flows such as India and the Philippines have seen increased interest in Bitcoin as a means to reduce fees and transfer times. Bitcoin-based remittance services like BitPesa and Coins.ph allow users to send funds abroad quickly and at a fraction of the cost compared to traditional methods. This has the potential to improve financial inclusion and help families in developing countries receive funds from abroad.

However there are challenges to widespread adoption of Bitcoin in cross-border transactions. Regulatory concerns such as anti-money laundering (AML) and know-your-customer (KYC) requirements can hinder the integration of cryptocurrencies into the global financial system. Additionally exchange rate volatility and liquidity issues can pose challenges for businesses and individuals seeking to rely on Bitcoin for cross-border transactions.

19.4 International Regulations and Treaties

Bitcoin operates in a global regulatory landscape that is still evolving. While some countries have embraced cryptocurrency and implemented regulatory frameworks to govern its use others have taken a more cautious or even hostile approach.

The lack of a centralized authority controlling Bitcoin poses challenges for regulators. The decentralized nature of the cryptocurrency makes it difficult to impose traditional financial regulations and enforce compliance. However regulatory efforts have been made to prevent money laundering terrorist financing and other illicit activities associated with cryptocurrencies.

Some countries have established clear regulatory frameworks to govern cryptocurrency exchanges and initial coin offerings (ICOs). For instance Japan has legalized Bitcoin as a form of payment and introduced a licensing system for cryptocurrency exchanges. Switzerland has also embraced cryptocurrencies through a regulatory approach that balances consumer protection with innovation.

On the international level organizations such as the Financial Action Task Force (FATF) have been working to establish global standards for cryptocurrency regulation. The FATF's guidelines aim to address areas such as customer identification AML and the sharing of cross-border transaction data. These efforts are essential for ensuring the integrity of the global financial system and preventing the misuse of cryptocurrencies for illicit purposes.

However achieving global consensus on cryptocurrency regulation remains challenging. Different countries have divergent approaches with some banning or heavily restricting cryptocurrencies while others are more permissive. As a result harmonizing regulations across borders and facilitating international cooperation remains a significant challenge.

19.5 Challenges in Developing Countries

While Bitcoin holds promise for financial inclusion in developing countries several challenges hinder its widespread adoption.

One of the key hurdles is the lack of internet access and digital literacy. Bitcoin relies on an internet connection and digital devices limiting its accessibility to those with the necessary infrastructure. In many developing countries internet penetration rates are low and a significant portion of the population lacks access to smartphones or computers. Addressing digital infrastructure gaps is crucial for expanding Bitcoin adoption.

Volatility is another challenge. Bitcoin's price can fluctuate dramatically making it challenging for individuals and businesses to rely on it as a stable medium of exchange or store of value. This volatility is particularly problematic for individuals in developing countries who are more likely to have limited financial resources. Stablecoins which are cryptocurrencies pegged to a stable asset like a fiat currency could provide a solution by reducing the impact of price volatility.

Additionally regulatory hurdles can impede Bitcoin adoption in developing countries. Lack of clear regulations or hostile stances by governments may deter businesses from accepting Bitcoin or hinder the development of local cryptocurrency

exchanges. Developing a regulatory framework that balances consumer protection with innovation is crucial for fostering cryptocurrency adoption in these regions.

Furthermore education plays a critical role in driving Bitcoin adoption. Many individuals in developing countries may be unfamiliar with cryptocurrencies or have misconceptions about their use and potential benefits. Educational initiatives should focus on raising awareness about Bitcoin blockchain technology and the opportunities they offer for financial inclusion and economic empowerment.

In conclusion Bitcoin's adoption varies across the globe influenced by economic geopolitical and regulatory factors. While some countries have embraced Bitcoin as a means of financial inclusivity and innovation others remain cautious or even hostile towards its integration into mainstream financial systems. Bitcoin has the potential to revolutionize cross-border trade and remittances offering fast and low-cost alternatives to traditional payment systems. However challenges such as regulatory frameworks internet access volatility and digital literacy hinder its widespread adoption particularly in developing countries. Overcoming these barriers will be crucial for maximizing the potential benefits of Bitcoin and blockchain technology on a global scale.

50 important tips

50 important tips to consider before buying Bitcoin:

1. **Educate Yourself**: Understand what Bitcoin is and how it works before investing.
2. **Start Small**: Especially if you're new to cryptocurrencies, begin with a small investment.
3. **Diversify Your Portfolio**: Don't put all your money into Bitcoin; diversify across different assets.
4. **Long-Term Perspective**: Consider Bitcoin as a long-term investment rather than a get-rich-quick scheme.
5. **Use Reputable Exchanges**: Only buy Bitcoin from well-known and trustworthy exchanges.
6. **Research Exchanges**: Compare fees, security measures, and user reviews when choosing an exchange.
7. **Secure Your Investments**: Use hardware wallets or secure software wallets to store your Bitcoin.
8. **Backup Wallets**: Always have backup copies of your wallet's private keys or recovery phrases.
9. **Beware of Scams**: Be cautious of phishing websites, fraudulent schemes, and fake giveaways.
10. **Two-Factor Authentication**: Enable 2FA on your exchange and wallet accounts for added security.
11. **Stay Informed**: Keep up with cryptocurrency news and developments.

12. **Understand Volatility**: Bitcoin prices can be highly volatile; be prepared for fluctuations.
13. **Risk Assessment**: Only invest what you can afford to lose; don't use borrowed money.
14. **Tax Obligations**: Be aware of your tax obligations related to Bitcoin gains.
15. **Avoid Emotional Trading**: Don't make impulsive decisions based on fear or excitement.
16. **Use Dollar-Cost Averaging**: Invest a fixed amount at regular intervals to reduce risk.
17. **Avoid Public Wi-Fi**: Don't access your wallet or exchange accounts on public Wi-Fi networks.
18. **Check Transaction Fees**: Be aware of transaction fees, especially during high network congestion.
19. **Verify Addresses**: Always double-check Bitcoin addresses before sending funds.
20. **Avoid FOMO**: Fear of Missing Out can lead to poor investment decisions; stay rational.
21. **Stash Funds Securely**: Keep your private keys and recovery phrases offline and in safe places.
22. **Peer Reviews**: Seek advice and insights from trusted peers in the crypto community.
23. **Use Secure Passwords**: Create strong, unique passwords for your accounts.
24. **Beware of Pump-and-Dump Schemes**: Avoid investing in assets hyped up for quick gains.
25. **Regulatory Compliance**: Ensure you comply with your country's cryptocurrency regulations.
26. **Hodl Wisely**: Don't panic-sell during market downturns; have a long-term strategy.
27. **Backup Everything**: Regularly backup your wallet and

account information.

28. **Analyze Market Trends**: Use technical and fundamental analysis for decision-making.

29. **Secure Your Email**: As it's often linked to your accounts, secure your email with 2FA.

30. **Privacy Coins**: Understand the features and implications of privacy-focused cryptocurrencies.

31. **Cold Storage**: Consider using cold storage methods for long-term holdings.

32. **Tax Reporting**: Keep records of your transactions for tax reporting purposes.

33. **Paper Wallets**: Learn how to create and use paper wallets securely.

34. **Crypto Community Forums**: Participate in reputable crypto forums to gain insights.

35. **Avoid Overtrading**: Frequent trading can lead to higher fees and losses.

36. **Research ICOs and Tokens**: If considering altcoins, research thoroughly.

37. **Don't Share Private Keys**: Never share your private keys with anyone.

38. **Test Small Transactions**: If trying a new wallet or service, start with a small test transaction.

39. **Understand Wallet Types**: Different wallet types (hot, cold, mobile) have varying security levels.

40. **Check Regulatory Updates**: Be aware of changes in cryptocurrency regulations.

41. **Crypto Taxes**: Consult with a tax professional if you have complex crypto holdings.

42. **Monitor Exchange Limits**: Check withdrawal and trading limits on your chosen exchange.

43. **Consider Hardware Wallets**: Hardware wallets provide high security for significant holdings.

44. **Avoid Impersonation**: Beware of social media accounts impersonating crypto influencers.

45. **Security Updates**: Keep your wallet and software updated with the latest security patches.

46. **Emergency Plan**: Prepare a plan for your loved ones to access your funds in case of an emergency.

47. **Risk Management**: Implement a risk management strategy to protect your investments.

48. **Back-Up Seeds**: Store wallet recovery seeds securely; they are your last resort.

49. **Review Your Strategy**: Regularly assess your investment strategy and adjust if necessary.

50. **Seek Professional Advice**: Consult with financial advisors or cryptocurrency experts if needed.